WINNING
THE WAR
ON WEEDS

WINNING
THE WAR
ON WEEDS

John Moody

CASTALIA HOUSE

Winning the War on Weeds

John Moody

Published by Castalia House
Tampere, Finland
www.castaliahouse.com

Cover Design: Castalia House

ISBN: 978-952-7065-42-6

Contents

What's the Matter with Weeds?   i

Part One: Weed Beating Boot Camp

1   Understand Your Enemy   3

2   Design a Powerful Defense   5

3   Manual and Chemical Weed Control   19

4   Eat Your Enemies   29

5   Weed Right: Prioritize your Targets   33

Part Two: Mulches

6   Bury your Weedy Woes and Foes   41

7   Wood-Based Mulches   53

8   Grass-Based Mulches   75

9   Living Mulches and Cover Crops   91

10 Man-Made Mulches: Metal, Plastic, and Repurposed   101

Part Three: Taking the Battle to the Weeds and Seeds

11 Organize Your Army!   117

12 Forced Germination   127

13 Solarization: Let the Sun do the Work for You   131

14 Occultation: One Tarp to Rule Them All   147

Part Four: Concentrated Weed Control

15 Flame Weeding   155

16 Steaming and Boiling Water   159

17 Animal Incorporation   163

Part Five: It's the End of the Weeds as We Know It

18 Understanding How Tools Impact Techniques and Tactics 171

19 Keeping the Weeds Away   175

Charts   181

About the Author   201

What's the Matter with Weeds?

Weed. The farmer's original four letter word. Nothing causes more headaches, backaches, and heartaches for gardeners than our many petaled, seeded, and rooted friends. They choke our cucumbers. They overrun our artichokes and asparagus. They invade our herbs and spices. Stealing sunlight, water, and nutrients, they may leave our gardens looking grim and growing poorly.

Those who grow food have always dealt with weeds and thus found ways to fight back. For most of human history it was through tillage and plowing, manual or animal in nature. This costly fight, in terms of labor and damage to land, would sometimes conquer or at least kowtow the weeds into a level of acceptable annoyance. Some cultures decided fire was the way to go, burning down areas to make space for annuals and other agriculture. This approach when done poorly had all sorts of deleterious impacts; when done properly, created incredibly fertile and sustainable landscapes. As we will see in later chapters, there are ways to harness heat in ways that our ancestors could not have imagined and that benefit our growing spaces and soil at the same time.

After World War II, the chemical leftovers of decades of conflict became the startovers of the new "green revolution" in agriculture. How the public was convinced that the chemicals that killed their fathers, husbands, and sons a few years before were okay to put on the food that would reach their dinner plates is beyond me. Yet it happened. In a few short decades, tillage and similar mechanical means of weed control were eclipsed by the unleashing of a vast chemical army to combat weeds. Now, hundreds of millions of pounds of pesticides—herbicides, fungicides, insecticides, and a plethora of other potentially toxic chemicals—are used in the US alone to grow food and maintain lawns and other landscaping. Glyphosate (Roundup) alone accounts for over three hundred million pounds per year.

While the amounts used have never been higher, the chemical army is losing. Resistant weeds are spreading. Soil health is suffering. Drift and overspray destroys thousands of adjoining farms, homesteads, and properties each growing season. It is a broken system with bitter results.

Tillage and chemicals, chemicals and tillage. People will say, "What else are we to do?" Are there better ways to control weeds? Yes, there are.

Our Story

When we began our homesteading and farming journey, I had limited experience growing things. The place we purchased had no established gardens or growing spaces. Just a bunch of non-organic matter, compacted lawns and pastures, full of grasses and weeds of every shape, size, and sort. Not just nice weeds, like dandelions, but noxious, hard to control species, like rhizome-reproducing thistles and slice-your-fingers-when-you-try-to-pull-it-up pigweed.

I tried tillage, but the soil broke the tiller before the tiller broke the soil. I tried sheet mulching, but weeds continued to push right through and overtake my garden. Some species, with the influx of fertility that our adding compost and other amendments created, even spread beyond their original limited spots! It didn't help that the fertility that I brought on farm—like composted cow manure from the local stockyards—contained enough weed seed to repopulate the entire eastern half of the United States! While we were making tremendous progress with our soil, going from below 1% organic matter to over 10%, we were losing the war with the weeds. Our gardens choked under their constant expansion.

In response, we upped our hand and tool weeding game. The kids and I would go out every week, a few times a week, for a few hours, pulling, slicing, ripping, shredding, and otherwise knocking back weeds. It was unenjoyable work, generally taking place at the most undesirable time of year—Kentucky's hot, humid mid to late summer. When the tiller broke, I realized that there was something wrong with this method of fighting weeds.

So, like with building soil, I started researching and then trying different approaches to weed control. Deep, organic mulches like straw and wood chips. Man-made mulches like black ag plastic and sheet metal. Living mulches and cover crops. Solarization, occultation, and forced germination. We tested and tried each method in many different ways, comparing our results with the results of other growers big and small.

Over the course of two years, we reduced our time spent weeding by around 80%. If you can imagine, everyone in our household was grateful and excited about the results. We also increased our crop yields and further improved our soil at the same time. We were finally winning the war against weeds. We want you to as well. We want you to understand and successfully apply a host of ways to fight weeds that don't require damaging the soil or exposing you and those who eat the food you grow to dangerous chemicals. Ways that don't undo your hard work building healthy soil so that you can have healthy plants that produce healthy food.

Who This Book is For and How to Use It

That is why you are here, true? You want to grow more and work less, especially work less with weeds! There are a few ways to use this book. First, realize, the sections are fairly independent of each other. Other than a brief intro to how the soil seed bank and weeds work and spread, every chapter is a stand alone adventure. You can skip right ahead to the section on mulches, then move back and read about edges and fences if you like. I won't care, since I already have your money and you have my book. At the end are various summary charts—you can just stick with those and ignore the rest if you are in a big hurry. No need to get bogged down in the nitty gritty details if that doesn't interest you. Instead, you can get right to weed annihilation if that is your pressing need and come back and read the rest later.

You may disagree with some of our conclusions or recommendations—that's okay, you won't hurt my feelings. Come find me online and let's talk about it. Take and use what you find helpful, discard or ignore the rest. Not every approach works or works the same on every farm and homestead—real life is complicated like that.

At the end of the book, I outline seasonal "work flows" for how different weed techniques are combined with various growing approaches. These are taken from our farm/homestead and a dozen or so other farms and operations I interviewed while writing this book. This allows you to see how particular weed control techniques outlined earlier in the book are implemented to grow particular crops with particular tools and approaches in particular places. It is one thing to know how to use a particular weed control approach, but another to know how to integrate it into the growing season, and yet another to see and understand how it fits into a year long flow of food growing that involves multiple crops passing through a single bed space.

I hope you will enjoy the book thoroughly and benefit from the research and work of so many growers who, like you, want to weed less, grow more, and get on to other exciting facets of homesteading and farming!

Also, I can't go any further without mentioning a few people. First, Dr. Steve Diver, a cover agricultural expert and crop specialist, and a friend, who contributed to many sections of this work directly and indirectly. Second, Sonja Birthisel, who is a professor specializing in occultation, solarization, and other things weed related. To Michael Leonido and David Good, my deep appreciation for reading the manuscript at various stages and giving so much helpful input and critique. To the many others who perused certain parts or otherwise contributed, my thanks. These and a number of other people not only have saved us time on our farm, but also their work and input probably saved this book from many errors! Our deepest appreciation for each of you.

There are an immense number of resources I consulted to help inform the information laid out in this book. First, to the many farmers and homesteaders I interviewed, thank you for your time and sharing your experiences. It doesn't matter how good something looks on paper if it doesn't work in practice in the field!

Pictures and Other Sundry Matters

You are probably wondering, "Where are the pictures?" I went back and forth, and eventually decided to put the pictures only on my website.

Why? Two reasons. First, color. The pictures are much better in color and for a number of sections, I have a large number of them. Color pictures are very, very expensive to put into a book, especially when I can have them on my website for free. Black and white just didn't seem to work. Second, cost. Pictures, especially color, double the cost of the book. They would also limit the total number of pictures I could have, unlike online where I can have full albums with as many pictures as I want for free. So, to save you money and to provide better quality and more helpful visuals, you will find most to all the pictures online. With that said, let's get on to getting rid of our weeds!

Part One

Weed Beating Boot Camp

1

Understand Your Enemy

If you know the enemy and know yourself, you need not fear the result of a hundred battles. If you know yourself but not the enemy, for every victory gained you will also suffer a defeat. If you know neither the enemy nor yourself, you will succumb in every battle.

—Sun Tzu

Before you can beat weeds, you need to understand them and and their life cycle. Soil has what is known as a "seed bank"—hundreds upon hundreds of years of built up, dormant seeds from innumerable species of plants. This seed bank combined with unwanted perennials is our adversary. Unlike your personal bank account, which you most likely desire to see increase, with the soil seed bank, you want to see it decrease. You want to have more withdrawals than deposits. More debits than credits. Generally, you want to get its balance as close to zero as possible. Also, you want to keep what is already in the seed bank from earning interest or increasing—by germinating, spreading, sprouting or otherwise coming back to life so it can reproduce and replenish the seed bank with more of its progeny.

Unfortunately, most growers grow in a way that not only damages their soil but also provides ample opportunities to make heavy deposits back into the seed bank. Tillage turns up buried seeds that otherwise would never see the light of day. Wind carries millions more invaders from the edges and adjoining places next to our growing spaces, replenishing or increasing the seed bank. Bare soil in our growing spaces invites these invaders to take up residence, take root, and eventually, reproduce. Monocultures of well spaced, isolated crops invite invasion into the emptiness around each plant. This requires additional rounds or tillage or cultivation, creating an endless cycle of weed wars. Sometimes the weeds get the upper hand, sometimes we do. But it never seems to end, because instead of winning the war, we are fueling it by how we manage our growing spaces.

Also, we are not alone in our battle against the soil seed bank. Many forces help reduce it. Birds, mice, and other animals and insects eat some of the seeds (but they also spread them as well!). Many seeds naturally lose viability over time. Material falls or moves over some, burying them too deep to ever again see the light of day unless nature or nurture disturbs their soil slumber.

Yet, none of these forces are enough to really knock back the seed bank alone. **Nature wants plant life to spread**. Bare spaces and tidy gardens are not part of its operating plan. We need to adjust our expectations for what a garden or growing space should look like. We also need to understand the forces that work to spread seeds and the tools available to remove unwanted plants that don't create endless cycles of work for us at the same time. That is what the rest of the book is all about—tools to work with, rather than against nature, to achieve a low to weed free growing space for you to enjoy.

2

Design a Powerful Defense

Growing spaces have numerous sources for weeds and weed seeds. First is the "seed bank," the built up accumulation of decades of weed seeds that have worked their way into the soil that we discussed above. Every disturbance of the soil—every time we till or dig or disturb the dirt, we awaken the dead. Innumerable seeds that have patiently waited to be resurrected by nature's or some human's or animal's actions.

Second, birds and other animals can carry weed seeds into our growing spaces. We can do some things to help stop this, but only so much. Thankfully, their addition is pretty easy to manage, especially if more difficult species they share, like some perennials, are caught early and quickly eradicated when they pop up.

Third, and more problematic for many growers, are wind and weather. This is perhaps one of the most underrated areas where growers can either help or harm themselves when it comes to weeds, and what we will focus on in this chapter. If we want to win against weeds, we need to design our growing spaces with victory in mind.

Last, actions growers take can greatly increase weed seeds and weeds in their gardens and growing spaces. Leaving bare ground, constant tillage, importing weed laden compost, and a number of other human actions can make weeds an inevitable issue. You reap what you sow, and many of us sow a great deal of weed seed and then wonder why we spend so much time weeding! In the last chapter we will discuss not undoing your hard work reducing the soil seed bank by foolish or otherwise imprudent decisions on your part.

Wind and Weeds

Most growing spaces are bordered by lawns, pasture, yards, or similar transitional spaces. These spaces provide the perfect place for unwanted plants to propagate and then infiltrate, carried along by wind and weather. Thus, it is important to map your growing space and understand the directions that incoming invaders will catch a wind or weather borne ride on. This map then helps you take steps to reduce incoming weed invaders.

Ways to reduce wind borne seeds include:

1. Plant windbreaks

Wind breaks were a common feature on farms for hundreds of years until recent times. Both larger windbreaks (trees) farther out from a growing space and shorter windbreaks (hedges, bushes, or other edible, medicinal, or aesthetic landscaping) closer in will lower overall wind speed. This reduces the distance seeds can travel, thus decreasing how much seed enters your growing spaces.

2. Create seed walls and transition spaces

Some amount of seeds will always try and hitch a ride into your garden. To help prevent their infiltration into our main growing area, we dedicated the west edge—an area about fifteen feet across that runs the length of the growing space—to trapping such invaders into a more easily maintained space by creating what I call a seed wall.

What does our transition space look like? At ground level along the fence, we are using comfrey, since it not only improves the soil and can take heavy mulching, but also attracts and provides early and late season food for pollinators, along with its compost and medicinal value. Next to the comfrey is a double row of blackberries. Again, these can take heavy mulching happily and are a high value addition to our growing space. Note how you can create a transition space that is productive, protective, and ecologically positive at the same time. This space provides food and medicine and animal fodder, while protecting our annual growing spaces just beyond effectively from incoming weed seeds, while also creating habitat for beneficial pollinators and predator species.

Also, every few years, the blackberry patch and other plants along the west edge take a beating during inclement weather that brings strong, damaging winds with it. They easily take the abuse and bounce back the following few months or season. Their sacrifice spares less able to endure, high value annual crops such as tomatoes, peppers, and the like in the main growing space. Windbreaks matter and can make a big difference to how many plants survive a bad storm. We have seen this first hand time and time again on our farm and many others. So understand that windbreaks are a worthwhile investment on many levels.

Chickens are occasionally moved through the space to fertilize, reduce any pest populations, and the like. This is easy to do using simple tools like portable poultry fencing, discussed later in the book. The sum total is the creation of a space that not only is productive in terms of food and medicine, but also protective of the rest of our growing space when it comes to weeds.

3. Keep adjoining spaces well mowed and trimmed

Once you have established good transition spaces and wind breaks, the next priority is to keep the adjoining areas well-mowed or mulched so that plants have little opportunity to go to seed or otherwise spread. We use both mechanical and animal means to accomplish this on our farm.

Rabbit tractors allow us keep the closest twenty to thirty feet well maintained. We also mow the adjoining fifty yards anytime it risks creating a large seed drop that may end up getting moved into our main growing space.

Keeping these adjoining areas and edges mowed down means far less work in our main growing space. It also lets our chickens lend a better hand at pest control, as well-mowed areas are easier for their daily pest patrol around the garden. In nature, avians follow ruminants for a reason—deep grass is harder for them to forage in and also poses more predator risk to your poultry. Mowing mimics nature when followed by a flock of chickens or other fowl.

When mowing, it is important to do so on **low wind days and to toss the plant debris AWAY from your growing space.** I can no longer count the number of times I have watched someone running their mower along their garden or some other growing space, tossing seed laden plant material right towards or into it! Some of these same folks I then had to listen to later complain about how much work weeding their garden always is…

We mow in a pattern that continually moves the plant matter farther and farther away from the edge of the growing space for about 10–15 yards. This may seem like common sense, but I have watched an uncommon number of folks on riding lawn mowers and similar equipment tossing plant matter into the air directly towards their gardens all too often, even if the first few, closest passes did push material away. Realize, a mower can throw plant matter 8–10 feet, and more powerful riding models can do double that. Add in some wind and you can see that not just a few passes, but a large swath needs to be mowed only away from your growing space to keep seeds out.

If you hire out such services, make sure they have the sense to not do the same.

Maintaining Paths

While solarization, occultation, and other techniques will help substantially reduce and remove weeds from paths, they will not keep the paths weed free nor make the paths user friendly. Some growers leave their paths in bare dirt, using manual or mechanical means to weed them every week or so during the season. This is less than ideal.

Bare dirt spreads disease, loses organic matter and other nutrients, erodes via wind and rain, and has reduced water and air holding capacity that benefits adjoining growing beds. Remember, bare dirt is bad. Our goal is to never see the ground in our growing spaces, especially as we close in on summer. So what do you do with paths?

Paths are a great place to build organic matter and soil for future use in your growing beds (or **as** growing beds—some growers will turn paths into beds, alternating their layout over time or rotating crops). Also, many plants in your beds or rows will push roots far out into the paths—healthy paths thus help create healthier crops with heftier yields in your main beds. With our paths, some are mulched (cardboard plus straw or wood chips).

Many are now in perennial cover crops like clovers. These naturally regenerate each year, while attracting pollinators and improving our growing area's soil. Sometimes we will combine these perennial clovers with additional mulch, usually added in the mid to late spring if needed. If a path shows signs of weed issues, we will hand weed or, if the problem seems severe, strip solarize it. This knocks back annual weeds with ease, but the perennial clovers will generally come right back in just a few weeks.

To help paths along with clover cover, we will often relocate plants that have taken up residence in growing beds into paths that need additional plant density to suppress weeds. This turns a negative task (having to remove a plant that is in the way) into a positive one (placing it somewhere that it will suppress weeds while attracting pollinators and supporting adjoining crop beds).

Whatever your approach, don't leave paths bare. Bare paths will require constant care, reduce your yields, increase pest issues, and create other problems. **Remember, bare space is a weed's best friend— either you will occupy it with something positive or neutral or they**

will make use of it instead. We never want to see bare ground—make sure it is mulched, either brown types or green (living) types or both!

Edges and Transition Spaces

Most growers have to deal with adjoining edges and other transition spaces. Many of us find our growing spaces bordered by lawns or pasture on one or more sides. Or perhaps your growing space goes right up to an adjoining property or parcel of land.

Along with having windbreaks and a seed wall, it is important to keep transition spaces under control weed wise. A pasture directly adjoining a produce field is always going to cause problems. If at all possible, you want to create a transition space or buffer zone between the two. Even just a 3–4 foot path will help immensely with grass and weed infiltration. Mulch, gravel, geotextile, a constantly mowed cover crop—it doesn't matter what the transition space is, but such a transition space is vital.

It is also important to think about how you and your equipment will get in and out of growing spaces. Such border paths and transition spaces make it much easier to move equipment in and out without importing lots of mud and muck and weed seed and debris. Do you have to cross long sections of grassy spaces first? Then you are going to pick up and relocate weed seeds along the way on your shoes, pants, and equipment wheels. So, if possible, try to create grass and weed free access to your growing spaces.

For us, our main growing space sits right next to a driveway. The entrances to the growing space are heavily mulched. The lawn/pasture side is planted to a seedwall of comfrey and blackberries. Farther out are windbreaks of elderberry bushes to further reduce the dominant incoming winds that could carry seed in from the lawn/pasture. The lawn and pasture closest to the growing space are kept well mowed to reduce seed head formation. Together, it makes an immense difference to the weed load in our growing space.

Fences

One of the major transition spaces that marks many growing spaces is fences. Many growing spaces require fencing because of deer and other animal pressure. The fence solves one problem—deer, rabbits, chickens and other critters can't get in to get your garden—but creates a different one. How do you keep them clear of grass and weeds?

These spots often become weed resistance headquarters, places where grasses and other unwanted plants often get out of hand. What are options to deal with them and keep them clear and in check?

1. Heavy mulch

Some growers keep their fences heavily mulched, making weeding easy and the amount of weed whacker or similar work in check. Such an approach may work well for you if you have a small enough space or access to sufficient mulching materials. At the same time, in our experience some weeds become real problems growing in a deep mulch along and under a fence. The fence makes it difficult to get at the roots without damaging the fence at the same time, so you can only constantly deal with the foliage, leaving the root intact, and thus facing constant resistance from the plant.

2. Metal mulch

A solution a friend used on their farm involved sheet metal underneath their fences. The sheets were about 20 inches wide, providing a 10-inch strip on either side of the fence, giving ample clearance for easy mowing. This protected their fence and saved a great deal of time, as the metal mulch will last as long or longer than the fence itself, so it added a little bit of upfront labor and cost for a great deal of long term savings.

If your cost per linear foot for 36 inch wide sheet metal is $2.00, when you cut the sheets in half that reduces it to $1.00. If your garden is 50x50 feet, that is a perimeter of 200 linear feet, so your total cost is

$220 dollars (to provide sufficient metal for overlapping the seams). If the metal lasts 10 years (it will last longer), this equates to a yearly cost of $22.00 to have a weed free fence area. Given that weed whacking the fence just once will take you an hour of time plus the cost of fuel and equipment, metal mulch seem like a great deal to me!

If you can get the sheet metal used, you will save even more. The only drawback? Used metal usually has small holes from where screws or other fasteners attached it to the structure. These holes will let some weeds grow through. These weeds will need dealt with, either by patching/sealing the holes or by manually weeding them as needed.

Another way to save money is to find a place that sells sheet metal and see what they charge for the cover sheets. Cover sheets protect the rest of the stack from any damage during transit and onsite storage until customer pickup. A few local businesses in my area end up with hundreds of these sheets a month and sell them at $1.00 or so a linear foot. They are a great deal and a great way to secure some brand new, hole-free metal mulch! They may have a scratch or ding, but the weeds don't seem to care.

Metal mulch under the fence thoughts

With metal mulch under a fence line, here are a few thoughts and pointers. First, most roofing metal comes in 36 inch wide sheets. You can easily cut these down to two eighteen inch sheets. This creates a 9-inch strip on each side of your fence. Also, the metal doesn't have to be centered under the fence. Perhaps you want more clearance on the grass/pasture side and less on the garden/growing space side, so you can do 12 out and 6 in, or even 14 out and 4 inches in. Experiment and see what works best for you and your equipment. I wouldn't go closer than 4 inches on the inside, as you want a nice easy edge to maintain, since you may need to occasionally trim along it with a weed whacker or similar tool.

Next, for your fence posts, should you drive them through the metal or in between the metal? The benefits of putting them through is that you create far less space for weeds to invade (weeds around posts are often a pain!). But if you put the posts through the metal, it makes removing the metal far more difficult and time consuming, since instead of just having to pull it out from under the fence, you have to remove the fence and pull the posts, or cut the metal. The other benefit of putting the posts through the sheet metal? It ensures the metal won't get airborne during high winds and bad weather.

On the balance, it is a better method to put the posts through the metal to help secure it in place. The easiest way to do this is use an angle grinder or similar tool to make a T-shaped hole to drive the post through. Remember that the two parts of the hole won't be equal in length. A T-post if it has the ground plate is much wider than it is deep.

A standard T-post is about three and a half inches wide and one and three quarters inches deep. So the cuts into the metal should be 4 inches by 2 inches. Make sure you orient the holes for the t-post properly in the metal so that the T-posts will face the right direction (generally facing out) for installing the rest of the fence!

Last, make sure the pieces of metal overlap sufficiently—go for 4–6 inches. Too little overlap and weeds will grow along, through, and in the gap where the pieces meet, pushing out quite easily and for some types, invading your growing space. If your ground is too uneven, you may need to place some weight on the seams, like a large rock or concrete block, to keep them tight and prevent weeds from using them as sheltered locations to grow.

3. Animal mowing

While mechanical mowing can damage fences or not adequately address weeds in small spaces, animal mowing can often maintain a fence fairly effectively. It won't completely remove the need to weed, but can significantly reduce your time and labor.

Both goats and sheep can do an excellent job of keeping a fence relatively clear. A mixed poultry flock—ducks, chickens, and geese, may also do a decent job or at least provide some work reduction. The challenge is using such animals in an efficient way that avoids any damage in your growing spaces, doesn't violate food safety rules for fresh animal manures, and doesn't take too much of your time. Having them mow solely from the outside protects your plantings inside and can reduce your work by half or more and is probably the best approach to take if you want to get animals into the garden weed control game. Fresh animal manures are a food safety risk and also may contain copious amounts of viable weed seeds, so allowing them into a growing space just isn't a good idea.

4. Edge trimmer/weed whacker or similar machine

Mechanical weed control is probably the most common method for maintaining a fence. It is also the most costly, especially in terms of time and labor.

Depending on the type of fencing, you need to exercise care so that you don't damage it when clearing vegetation. Almost all modern edge trimmers create enough force to easily bend and even break welded wire and similar fencing materials. Thus, proper care is crucial when using power tools to clear fencing.

One way to make your fences less prone to damage by mechanical grass and weed removal is to install bottom boards on one or both sides of the fence. These are usually made with 1x4 to 1x8 inch wooden rails attached along the bottom edge of the fence. This creates a durable, straight edge to mow or trim against while offering protection to the wire that sits behind or between the boards.

The type of wood and other factors will impact how rot-resistant and long lasting it is, or if you treat it with any preservative or wood protectant. Remember, not all of these treatments are safe or allowed for growing spaces or soil, especially if you are certified organic or certified naturally grown.

5. Trenching

If time and budget allow, another way to make a fence area weed free and also exclude and eliminate some pests—especially rodents like voles and moles—is by creating a trench under the fence that is then lined with a geotextile (optional) and filled with rock. The trench should be about 8–12 inches wide and a foot or more deep at the center. If you take this approach, make sure you use a HIGH GRADE, durable geotextile under the rock if at all. Our personal experience having to pull out and remove low grade geotextiles installed by previous owners in other applications resulted in pull-your-hair-out frustration! The fence is then installed over top the trench or even down into the trench and then the lower part of the fence buried to help exclude pests.

Another option, especially to deal with rabbits and a few other digging critters, is instead of burying the fence, to bend the bottom outer 6–12 inches and lay it facing out from the growing space. Think of it as turning your fence into a giant L shape, with the bottom edge pointing out and away, making it hard for digging critters to get under and into your growing space. The benefit of this approach is that the buried fence material, depending on your climate, begins to break down fairly quickly, so the bottom buried portion of the fence may only last three to five years before you need to replace it. The bent fence will not last as long as upright fence, but much, much longer than its buried counterpart.

A trench such as the above can also be maintained by steaming, boiling water, flame, or similar control methods to remove any weeds that do push up and through the rock. Since a well made trench should face much lower weed pressure, you should look at a trench as an up-front investment in protecting a growing space both from below ground pests and as a transition space to help eliminate weeds.

Other Fence Maintenance Methods

There are many additional ways to deal with fences. Some growers will use boiling water, steam, flame weeding, or chemicals to control their fence lines. All these methods have particular costs, challenges, and drawbacks, some of which we will discuss in later chapters. Some, like steam or boiling water, may be useful for spot treatment of a problematic fence area that is otherwise maintained through one of the methods outlined above. For instance, a deeply mulched fence may need flame or steam weeding on occasion, especially for particular spots or plants that pose a problem. View maintaining your fence lines similar to maintaining your growing spaces—even if you employ one or two major approaches to beating back the weeds, don't be afraid to bring in an additional tools when it makes sense for a particular pest or problem.

A Final Option: Portable Fencing

One other option worth mentioning with fences is for those who want to invest the additional money (and labor), portable, electric net fencing is another approach. There are two methods I have seen growers use—first, rotating paddocks around the outside of the growing space.

Second, creating a narrow space that circles the entire growing area. This creates an alley for cows, chickens, ducks or other animals to graze and wander in around the growing space while also working fairly well as a deer deterrent at the same time. The animals will help keep the space grazed. Also, they may help protect it from some types of pests. When necessary, the fencing is removed and any weeds in the area controlled by other methods, generally mowing.

This approach doesn't scale well. Most of the growers I have seen use it are protecting rather small growing spaces—generally a half acre or so at most, and more often much less. Sometimes they are larger, and use this approach along a single edge or area adjacent to a growing space.

Such a method definitely requires more labor and may not be viable for larger growing spaces or even all the sides of a smaller or moderately sized space. If you are moving animals anyway, it may be an effective solution for your situation, as it has been for a few farmers and home-steaders I know. **If it helps reduce deer pressure and damage to your growing space**, then this approach is especially enticing given the many benefits—producing and protecting food at the same time!

3

Close Quarters Combat: Manual and Chemical Weed Control

While this book focuses on non-chemical and non-tillage based weed control, there are a few approaches and options worth mentioning. There are also a few times that using hand tools and getting our hands dirty is necessary or makes sense.

Hand Weeding

While the tools we outline in this book go a long way to reducing your weed work, at the end of the day, some will still remain and survive. There will always be stragglers to deal with. We use a few different tools for hand weeding. For deep-rooted perennials, we have a standing weed puller made by Fiskars. It is useful for dealing with early season perennials like dandelion and dock, or for helping finish off other kinds of plants after solarization or occultation.

A hand and standing scythe are quite helpful in some settings. For instance, they let you easily weed back a space where you will then use mulch or solarization. Or, they can let you cut back a cover crop or understory that is getting a little too tall or aggressive around your main planting. Such tools are especially nice for raised beds or other small spaces where bringing in a lawn mower or other even small equipment doesn't make sense.

One of our favorite tools is a long handled trail tool made by SHW. This lets us reach and remove small weeds without having to bend. Eliot Coleman helped design and popularize a collinear hoe that is very useful for larger spaces, and a stirrup hoe can be another useful addition to your occasional hand weeding weaponry. In very large spaces, consider moving up to a wheel hoe/wheeled weeder.

While we used to have to use these hand tools to maintain our growing spaces, we now find we need them less and less as we have gotten the weeds under control. But they are still good to have on hand and most serve other purposes around our homestead, so they are worth having around.

The Claw: A most useful hand tool for perennials

A few years ago, after hearing mixed reviews, I decided to purchase a claw weeder. This tool allows you to pull a wide variety of weeds—like plantain, dandelion, and many others—without bending down. One reason it receives mixed reviews is that it takes a bit of practice to learn to use it properly and it is hard to use effectively in some soil types. If your soil is very hard clay, it doesn't do nearly as well as in looser, more easily worked situations.

This tool is especially helpful for removing perennials like dandelion and dock. While you will not get all the roots, it lets you remove nice size chunks at a time, which thus lets you take out a large amount of root/plant energy reserves quickly. Coupled with occultation or solarization, a claw weeder can help you make much quicker and easier work of many otherwise difficult and time consuming to deal with weeds.

Cultivation vs. Tillage

Especially for some crops and growing beds, occasional light cultivation may serve as the best weed control option. What is the difference between cultivation and tillage? Depth. Around 80–90% of seeds that become weeds are in the top two or so inches of the soil. Hence why mulch is so effective at reducing many types of annual weeds—it moves them from an inch or so from light and air to many, many inches below, where they no longer want or can become plants. But some crops don't do well with mulches, and some soil or situations don't work well with them either.

When we cultivate, we seek to turn up just the seeds in the top 1–2 inches of soil. You can do cultivation in smaller beds or spaces with a good garden rake (not leaf rake!). For larger growing spaces, more formal cultivation tools such as wheel hoes and the like make a good investment.

Cultivation leads us to a very old form of weed control, and one that is very important and useful for some crops—creating stale or false seeds beds.

Stale and False Seeds Beds

Imagine if you could eliminate 90% of possible weeds in just a few weeks? This is the goal of creating false or stale seed beds. The process is relatively simple.

First, a seed bed is prepared and the top 1 to 2 inches of soil cultivated to bring up weed seeds. Then, the bed is watered (if needed) to help encourage germination. After 1–2 weeks—long enough for a large number of the seeds to germinate—the new weedlings are killed. The method by which they are removed determines if the seed bed is considered stale or false.

What is the difference between a false and stale seed bed?

While often used interchangeably, stale and false seed beds are achieved through slightly different methods.

Stale seed bed—weeds are killed through solarization, occultation, flaming, steaming, herbicide treatment, or a combination of these techniques. Sometimes the crop is sown **before** the weeds are killed.

False seed bed—weeds are killed through another round of cultivation, creating the final, true seed bed (the first seed bed wasn't the true, final seed bed, hence why it is called false).

Note that with a false seed bed, it is critical that the second round of cultivation is done at exactly the right depth—too deep, and it will turn up additional weed seeds, ruining the now semi weed free bed.

With a stale seed bed, timing of occultation or flaming is the critical component to success—too late and the weeds will be too well established to easily kill off. Too early and many may still not have germinated.

Drawbacks and challenges to false and stale seed beds

The above sounds simple, right? Then what is the catch that makes this technique less popular or widely used given its fairly effective success rate? First, the technique depends on timing and weather. If winter goes long, you may lose the window to use this technique before you need to get plants in the ground. The soil needs adequate moisture and sun/warmth to create the ideal conditions to cause a flush of weeds to all emerge during the same window so that they can all then be removed **at the same time** as well. The amount of time it takes to apply this technique can create issues. For instance, field studies have shown that twenty to thirty days are needed to achieve optimal results before planting or transplanting many crops.

Second, especially if you use cultivation to kill the weeds, you have to do it just right and at just the right time or you will turn up or leave behind a large number of weeds to deal with later. Third, if you are plagued by certain types of weeds, especially ones that are slow to germinate or many mixed species that germinate at variable rates, this can radically reduce the success of such a technique.

The main solution to these challenges and drawbacks is found by marrying false or stale seed beds to other weed control options—

especially occultation and forced germination—which we will discuss later in the book.

Chemical Weed Control the Organic Way

There are a number of natural chemicals that you may consider using to help control weeds. Unlike modern herbicides, many of these were used historically and none have issues with bioaccumulation in the soil if you use good quality products. They do have benefits and drawbacks, so let's look at the major options.

Horticultural vinegar

Unlike standard, store bought vinegar, which is only so-so at best for knocking back weeds, some growers use what is known as horticultural vinegar. Standard vinegar runs around 3–7% acidity. At higher, concentrations, such as 10–20% acidity, vinegar is fairly effective against a wide range of weeds, mainly broadleaf. These higher concentration products are sometimes called horticultural vinegar. They are also fast acting (treated plants perish within 24 hours of application).

Note, vinegar's effectiveness against grasses is quite low, regardless of concentration. Also, its overall effectiveness is rooted in early application—small, newly germinated (within past two weeks, plants that have less than five leaves formed), fast growing plants are most affected. Large, well established plants may be knocked back by an application or two, but not killed. Same with deep rooted perennials. Plants that in field trials are most susceptible include broadleaf plantain, carpetweed, common chickweed, cutleaf evening primrose, ground ivy, oriental mustard, pale smartweed, tumble pigweed, spiny amaranth, lamb's quarters, velvetleaf, and recently germinated crabgrass. Similar plants to these, such as Creeping Charlie, are most likely also susceptible.

On the plus side, vinegar does not bioaccumulate nor alter soil pH. So it doesn't pose a long term risk to soil or plants. Interestingly, while most weeds are impacted by 10% acidity and above vinegar applications, some crops, like corn, are not. So with vinegar tolerant crops, if the weed issue is right, vinegar may make a good option for dealing with young weeds among the planting. Note, for CNG and organic certification, you can only use vinegars derived from plant sources, instead of those created by chemical reactions.

While you don't need specialized equipment, a handheld or backpack sprayer is necessary to safely and effectively apply vinegar. **Great care is needed when handling and spraying vinegar**. You can easily suffer chemical burns via spills, splashes, or spray drift. Like with other chemicals, during light to high winds, you may end up damaging off-target, bystander plants. Consider ag vinegar as extremely dangerous to both you and any other plants near the application areas.

Horticultural vinegar is also fairly expensive—around $20–30 a gallon. Given that it is only moderately effective and often requires multiple applications, we rarely use it anymore, preferring other simpler and safer approaches. Some growers in some regions have found it to be a cost effective approach to controlling certain weeds. One place that vinegar is highly effective? Helping keep gravel roads, outdoor patios, cracks, and similar spots clear.

For small spaces, a handheld steam unit is probably a much better choice, though. Cost wise, these units are now under $100 and can easily handle keeping paths, small beds, and other spots weed free.

Essential and other oils

Clove, citrus, garlic, and many other plant based oils are also semi-effective herbicides. Usually, they are added to a vinegar, soap, or epsom salt based spray to boost its plant killing power. Thus, they have the same drawbacks mentioned above with vinegar. Studies show fairly mixed results when using essential oils at larger scales, even when combined with other adjuvants to try and improve their effectiveness.

Oils may have side benefits, such as some pest and disease control potential and other beneficial impacts on some plants. They also have drawbacks, especially off-target harm to beneficial insects and other garden dwellers. Also, they are relatively costly, especially when applied to larger areas—many are used at rates of 25–50 gallons per acre, where the essential oil is 10% or more of the application mixture. A single gallon of some essential oils quickly runs into the mid-multiple hundreds of dollars.

Here is the cost per gallon for some common herbicidal essential oils, non-organic.

- Clove: $500–800
- Thyme: $500–700
- Cinnamon: $200–300

I think it is best summed up with this quote:

Common conclusions drawn from these studies were that none of the essential oil herbicides provided any residual weed control, small weed size was critical for maximum efficacy, environmental conditions affected herbicide performance, and rates necessary for maximum efficacy made the treatment costly.

http://horttech.ashspublications.org/content/24/4/428.full

I am not saying don't use or try essential oils, just that our experience and the research shows that there are better, less costly, more reliable alternatives currently available.

Soaps

Soap is often added to both natural herbicides and pesticides to improve contact and coating, break down plant and bug defenses, and improve the overall effectiveness of the mixture. Ever notice how on some plants, water forms beads that easily run right off? The plants exude various protective chemicals that coat their foliage. Soap helps break down that protective coating, allowing the other components of the mixture to adhere and attack the underlying plant tissues effectively.

If you are going to use a soap, I recommend only using natural, high quality products such as Dr. Bronner's or similar. Remember, whatever you apply to your plants will eventually make it into your soil. Whatever makes it into your soil may well end up in your plants. What ends up in your plants ends up in you!

Combination products

Many products are now made using a combination the above ingredients, including additional ingredients such as salts (usually epsom). Combination products tend to have higher rates of effectiveness. Also, some have formulas aimed at dealing with a particular weed or weed species, which will make them more useful for those who need a particular control for a particular problematic plant. Like the above, they still suffer from issues with effectiveness, cost, and application dangers.

Example recipe

- 1 gallon horticultural vinegar
- 2 cups epsom salts
- 1/4 cup dish soap (I prefer Dr. Bronner's liquid soaps—some contain essential oils that that may help improve the effectiveness of the mixture)

Pre-emergents: cornmeal based weed controls

A pre-emergent is a herbicide that seeks to inhibit seed germination. Aka, it stops a weed before it starts. The most common, natural one is cornmeal based. Studies show mixed field results in terms of effectiveness.

Also, note that they will not harm or hinder existing plants! These products are pre-emergent herbicides only—that is they can only stop some plants before they get started. Once something is growing, they provide no benefits whatsoever. All they can do is stop seeds from germinating.

While they will not stop all plants from germinating, they are fairly effective (85% or so) against a number of pesky weeds, such as chickweed, crabgrass, and dandelions. They are usually made from GMO corn and may contain other fillers or be combined with other chemicals, so make sure you thoroughly check the labels so you know exactly what you are putting in your growing spaces! If you have certain certifications, don't assume these products are permitted or allowed before you try them.

Final notes on chemical approaches to weed control

So, can chemical based controls help or work against weeds? To some extent yes. Are they cost and labor effective? Generally and at least currently, no. Numerous studies show that compared to standard chemicals, you are looking at substantial cost increases—**anywhere from three hundred to two thousand percent**. The good news? For the most part, if you manage weeds with other techniques and tools we cover, you won't really need to use these controls with their additional costs and labor anyway. Instead, it is best to save that money and invest in bio and other mulches, a portable, handheld steam weed sprayer or flame weeder, or other, more cost effective tools and options that make sense for the size and scale of your operation.

On a rare occasion, we may have a situation where a small application of horticultural vinegar or some other organic mixture may make sense to take care of a small patch of some sort of pesky weed or invasive that for whatever reason, we can't use solarization or some superior technique against. That is the key, at least for me—we have better tools and alternatives, so why bother with these? Honestly, we haven't used many of these in years, since we have moved on to better, safer, less costly and easier to use approaches.

4

Eat Your Enemies

Many weeds are the most nutritious foods you will find in your garden or growing spaces. Dandelions and lamb's quarters bodyslam lettuce and spinach, nutritionally speaking. Chickweed comes early, a green you can eat long before any are ready in your garden. Just look at these comparisons.

For instance, let's compare spinach, often hailed as a superfood, to nettle. Per ounce, spinach contains around 28 milligrams calcium, 24 magnesium, and 167 potassium. Nettle? 970 calcium, 286 magnesium, and 583 potassium. Dandelions, a well beloved native American food that most modern people treat as a hated weed, contain seven times more phytonutrients than spinach. They also contain almost twice as much calcium, three times the vitamin A, five times the vitamin K and E. Oh, and organic dandelion greens don't cost $16 a pound, you can just go pick them outside in your grass or growing spaces for free!

Lamb's quarter—also known as wild spinach—is another worth highlighting. It contains 2 to 4 times the phytonutrients of spinach, 15 times the calcium, 8 times the vitamin C, and more of many other nutrients. We could go on and talk about purslane and dozens of others. But hopefully you get the point—wild plants are incredibly nutritious, and many grow with absurd ease.

Depending on the size of your garden or growing space, eating or even selling all the weeds may not be an option, though many of these greens can make great additions to salad and other mixes. Yet, it can make a significant dent both in their population and in your food budget, especially by providing some greens early in the season when your garden ones are still weeks or months away! Learn to love the right kinds of weeds. Eat them early. Eat them often!

Please note that proper identification of wild plants is very important so you don't poison yourself or your loved ones. If you are unsure, get assistance to ensure accurate identification, especially for any plants that in your area have doppelgangers of the poisonous kind. Also, almost all edible plants are more palatable when young, and **generally** don't require cooking, especially in small amounts added to salads or other dishes. As plants mature, the leaves often become more fibrous, tough, or strong tasting, and most to all benefit from or require cooking before consumption. It is best from a weed management perspective not to let the plants reach this stage anyway, so hopefully you will have eaten or otherwise disposed of plants before they become both unappetizing and a possible weed reproduction problem in your growing space!

Early Season/Spring

- Chickweed
- Dandelion
- Hen's Bit
- Creeping Charlie
- Hairy bittercress

Mid Season/Summer

- Clover, especially red (blossoms are great in tea)
- Lamb's quarter
- Wood Sorrell

- Purslane
- Curly dock
- Burdock
- Yellow dock
- Chicory
- Plantain
- Queen Anne's Lace
- Pigweed (when very young only)
- Mallow
- Nettle

Late Season/Fall

New growth of any mid-season plants (many become unpalatable as they mature, and many also develop plant based toxins that apart from cooking or other preparation make them more problematic). Depending on your location, many early season weeds may make a reappearance on the dinner plate in the fall! In our area, they tend to reappear in late October and early November.

Note, this list isn't comprehensive, it just touches on ones we commonly see and use and that occur in much of the United States. Numerous excellent books, especially those by Samuel Thayer, are worth acquiring if you plan to incorporate wild and foraged foods into your daily or weekly diet. They are also well worth the investment.

5

Weed Right: Prioritize your Targets

Not all weeds are created equal. Lamb's quarter is slow to seed, but prolific once the cooler fall weather comes and it senses winter's approach. Thistles reproduce not just by seed, but by root (rhizomes), which, when cut into pieces, proliferate into dozens of more plants instead of dying. Oh, and they do it all summer into fall as well. Some grasses are slow growers and stay put, while others grow swiftly, seed early and often, and spread aggressively.

If you have a large garden but limited time, you may have to prioritize your weeding if you want to win. Not all weeds are created equal and not all require equal care and concern, especially in paths or other places. You also have to remove them in the right way so you don't accidentally cause them to multiply.

Early Season Occultation, Mulch, Hand and Tool Weeding

Weed control early season focuses on occultation, some hand weeding (mainly for chickweed in particular, troublesome spots), and a trust that our coming summertime solarization will continue to reduce a few troublesome, early season varieties.

Apply early season mulch with extreme care—while it generally helps immensely with weed issues, it can create a number of problems if not done properly. We mulch areas that are relatively weed free to keep them that way, and we generally do so in late spring so that the mulch doesn't delay soil warming or trap in excess spring moisture. We will also heavily mulch paths that don't show any problematic weed species, sometimes placing down cardboard first to significantly improve the mulch's success.

Not mulching is especially important for any early season weeds that you accidentally let seed. Since the seeds are left on the soil's surface, proper solarization sterilizes the bulk of them. It is best not to let them seed, but if they do, as long as you don't bury them solarization can undo most to all the damage and help break the weed cycle.

Slow Seeders Can be Mown or Otherwise Controlled

With lamb's quarter and other plants that are slow to seed, these can be allowed to go along until an opportune time to mow or otherwise remove a large number presents itself. Note that with lamb's quarter and a few others, going too long and allowing the plants to become too large will make them very woody, and thus harder to mow or remove. Try to mow them back at the still moderately young and supple stage. We will often let lamb's quarter act as a free cover crop on paths and other places, since it is also a nutritious and delicious free food as well.

Rhizomes require a war of attrition

If you are facing rhizome reproducers, tillage and any other methods that chops up underground plant material will almost always make the problem worse. The best way to beat these back is through a war of attrition. Plants store energy in their root systems. Every leaf they grow represents lost energy. That energy isn't limitless—so with rhizome reproducers it is just a matter of using up their energy before they use up yours! Any method that defoliates them will work— occultation, solarization, and more. If your soil tilth permits, pulling up some root material and making sure it expires because of exposure to sun will speed up the process significantly. A few inches of root system represents many dozens or hundreds of leaves! Combined with solarization and other suggestions outlined in the book, you should get any perennial rhizome reproducers under control in under a few months. A claw weeder is an excellent help if you have many large rooted perennails to remove.

Beware of grass

One common mistake I see with grasses comes when they are weeded, but not removed, because no seed head is visible on the stalks. Grasses may contain a large number of viable seeds inside the sheath long before these are visible to the sun. Grasses should be kept in check as soon and as early as possible for this reason. **Always prioritize grasses!** Older plants should not be composted but used to fertilize pasture or other places where seed inclusion won't matter. Always assume grass and grass clippings contain viable seeds. Always assume that they contain LOTS of viable seeds at that!

Don't give up too soon

When we first started, we struggled against pigweed and thistle. The pigweed was introduced through composted cow manure and was also naturally present on our land (remember, composting is no guarantee that the final product is weed free; always do an assay!). The thistle was already well established. Both now make nary an appearance anywhere in our growing space, requiring maybe at most one to two hours over the entire growing season to remove stragglers or new invaders.

Don't bury the weeds!

A number of techniques we will explore later in the book can take care of spots with large numbers of weed seeds. So, if an area gets out of hand, don't make the problem worse by hiding your mistake with mulches. Let the seeds fall and use the tools we outline later to take care of them. Mulching or burying areas with fresh, large seed drops helps protect the seeds from other methods of weed seed removal and reduction.

In summary, the types of weeds that you should prioritize the highest are:

1. Perennial rhizome reproducers—thistle, anyone?

2. Quick and strong spreaders—Bindweed, mint and similar plants should be strictly controlled

3. Those that reproduce by both seed and root, especially heavy seeders (like pigweed!)

4. Grasses of all kinds, because they produce such large amounts of seed and do so repeatedly during the season

Bucket and sheet metal disposal

We usually keep a bucket or two or some pieces of sheet metal around our growing spaces. This means we are never too far from a place to dispose of weeds properly. The sheet metal is great especially from late May through end of August. We can toss appropriate seed free weeds onto it or rhizome roots and allow the sun to quickly kill them. For things that may contain seeds, they go into the buckets and these buckets are dumped into areas of pasture or other places that could use the additional nutrients or need reseeded because of erosion or other issues. Thus, the task of weeding accomplishes two goals—weed reduction and pasture improvement/renovation.

We don't compost weedy material from the garden for reintroduction later. Over the years, we have found it just isn't worth the risk. Most people way overestimate their composting ability, and thus, often are importing the children and grandchildren of the weeds they just spent so much time and energy removing from their growing space. With so many free compost inputs available—coffee grounds, pitch produce, animal manures, and more—using a relatively low value high weed risk input just doesn't make any sense to me.

Assaying Compost for Weed Load

Speaking of compost, how do you know if compost is relatively weed free or a Trojan horse, a seeming gift that is actually full of war-ready weeds inside? There are a few steps we take.

1. Visit the place you are getting compost from—we visually inspect the compost piles at different stages of production. Are there weedy, unkempt spots close by, especially that winds would carry seed from? Many of those seeds are going to end up in the compost piles. Are the piles weed free and looking good and hot at the right stages of the process? How are finished piles protected from weeds and how long and old are they before they make it off the location?

2. Assay the compost—there are two benefits to assaying your compost. First, you will find out how weedy it is. Second, you can at the same time see if it suffers from any herbicide contamination.

How to assay

1. Get two or so gallons of compost.

2. Cut the compost with potting mix or similar **sterile** growing medium. A weed-free medium is crucial to ensure accurate results.

3. Place some of the mix two or so inches deep in a container in a warm sunny place, like a clear plastic tote or bin. You can, if wanting to check for herbicides at the same time, plant green beans or similar fast growing plants into the mix at a very low density (six or so plants for a half square foot). Just make sure you set up a control planting of the same seeds to ensure that the seeds are not the problem or some other factor if doing an herbicide assay at the same time.

4. Add water as needed. Observe what happens over 14–21 days. The more green you see (other than your possible addition of beans or a similar, purposeful planting), the more free weed seed is going to come along with your compost.

Part Two

Mulches

6

Bury your Weedy Woes and Foes

Mulching is simply covering the soil with some sort of material. There are many approaches to mulching. A grower can use organic (that is, carbon based) mulches—straw, hay, leaves and the like. These are often also referred to as bio or biological mulches. For bio mulches you have two main types. First is tree based, from wood chips and sawdust to leaf mold and bark mulch. Second is grass/plant based, which encompasses all the different types of hay and the various kinds of straw.

Some growers use non-organic mulches, such as food growing approved black plastic or geotextiles. A few go even further, using sheet metal and similar long lasting materials to keep weeds locked away from sun and air. The next few chapters will give you an in-depth look at mulches—how to source, how to use, and what to watch out for with each kind.

Don't Let Mulch Unleash Mayhem

While mulch has many benefits, it also has a number of risks. Think of it as a possibly, but not usually, unreliable ally—as long as you do your due diligence, it will serve you well.

Unwanted weeds and seeds

Both hay and straw may contain grass and weed seeds. While hay will **always contain a fair bit of weed seed**, improperly harvested straw can also cause trouble. We avoid hay mulch for this reason—it is a treadmill for weed control. Once you hop on, it is really hard to get off. Every year of hay mulch means that much more built up seed bank in the soil below. Our goal is to draw down that bank account to near zero, not provide it with a monthly deposit! There are a few exceptions to a heyday of seeds—like high quality alfalfa hay—but as a general rule I stay away from hay mulch.

While hay is seed heaven, straw and other mulches may also contain various seeds and weeds, so it is best to inspect and test them before you purchase. Generally, the main seed contamination is caused by improperly harvested crops, where some of the grain gets left behind. You can on occasion get a nice, free cover crop this way, or a potato bed overrun by wheat grass!

Persistent herbicides

While weeds may keep you awake at night, herbicides are what you should really be concerned about. Many new herbicide formulations are far more damaging and persistent than ones from previous decades. Small amounts (parts per billion) can cause years of damage to your growing spaces. The worst, aminopyralid and clopyralid, have long half lives and wide arrays of plants they impact. These may end up in both hay and straw, along with animal manures and composts. You cannot be too careful when making sure any inputs you bring on farm are free from these chemicals. I now know over a handful of growers who lost growing spaces for multiple years because of contaminated mulch or compost. Tens of thousands of additional reports of plant damage occur across the US each year.

There are also now reports that tree based mulches may contain chemicals that harm garden plants. It is good, if you are getting wood based mulches from tree companies, especially those that maintain the power lines in your area, to ask if they use any sprays or other chemicals on the trees.

Want less weeds, larger yields, and lots more nutrients? Mulch!

As a final way to try and encourage you to make use of mulches, especially organic bio mulches, they are about far more than just weed control. A number of studies show that mulches not only increase yields, but they also increase the nutritional value of the crops you grow. Talk about a perfect trifecta to get motivated to move mountains of mulch! In many of the studies, the yield increases are quite substantial—you are looking at a 20–30% increase in harvest!

The Many Methods of Mulch

One thing you will rarely see in nature, save where people or sudden calamities have happened, is bare soil. Exposed, barren earth isn't the natural state of the stuff beneath our feet. If on occasion land is rendered uncovered, things move quickly to remedy the problem. Like how our bodies don't tolerate open wounds, but fill and seal or risk unwanted invaders taking up residence, so ecosystems seek to fix scars and other such happenings that expose the earth beneath. Whether organic debris or living plant-life of ten thousand kinds, adapted to cover and make use of even the tiniest of spaces and places, nature abhors a vacuum.

Yet, much of modern agriculture is built around rejecting this basic premise. Growers tend to rip open the soil, then fight nature through machines and man-made chemicals to keep it that way. To undo all the forces of nature comes at a heavy price.

Sustainable and organic growers know there is a better way to reduce competition for crops yet not leave the soil unprotected—mulches. Mulches can take many forms. We have divided them up into three main categories. First, organic mulches. These are carbon (plant life) based mulches that feed the soil as they protect it. Second are living mulches, plants that can coexist with others without competing with them. Last are inorganic mulches. These are handiwork of man, made to somewhat mimic nature or remnants of other applications repurposed to suppress weeds.

Nature abhors a vacuum. Farmers don't fancy weeds. Mulching is about finding a balance between the two extremes. As we have mentioned previously, bare soil is like a bad wound. An untreated, uncared for wound can lead to serious complications—infection, scarring, even death. The same is true with bare soil.

Such soil is subject to erosion, compaction, organic matter depletion, and invasive species expansion. Bare soil doesn't happen often in nature, and when it does, nature works quickly to reestablish itself in the open spaces, like skin that works to quickly regrow over an open wound. Unfortunately, the regrowth of nature often involves the establishment of invasive or other unwanted species.

Mulch is the grower's solution to protecting bare spaces—it is nature's band-aid for bad wounds, giving soil (or the soil steward) time and opportunity to heal the exposed land. There are three approaches to mulching that we will cover in the following four chapters. First, organic mulches—organic here meaning carbon based mulches that are tree or grass based. Next, we will look at living mulches, also known as cover crops. Last, we will look at manmade mulches—landscape fabric, geotextiles, and other options.

Why Mulch?

Mulching helps address three major issues growers face. When bare soil is exposed, erosion caused by wind and rain follows. Mulches protect soil from erosion by buffering the effects and absorbing the energy of wind and rain. It also stops the top layer of soil from drying out and turning to particles and dust that then blow or wash away.

Bare soil exposed to direct sunlight and air volatilizes—the organic matter and many other compounds quite literally get "burned" out of the soil, going from ground to gas! Mulches shade and protect the soil from this highly damaging "sunburn." We would never leave our kids outdoors in the summer for a single sunny day beyond a few hours (or sometimes even minutes!). Why do we then think that our soils will do fine when exposed to such intense sunlight for an entire growing season? Mulch is like SPF 100 protection for our precious soil.

Even better, these three forces—sunlight, wind, and rain—are exactly what a grower wants applied to organic mulches, as it is what helps break them down into high organic matter soil. So what serves as a bane to bare or exposed soil is a blessing to a deeply bedded mulch. In healthy systems, mulches will break down in one to two growing seasons, adding an incredible amount of organic matter while feeding important parts of the soil food web.

Second, bare soil's water retention and total water holding capacity is reduced, especially over time, as it heats and then contracts, squeezing air and water out of the soil. This repeated process creates significant compaction, with reduced water and air holding capacity. Mulches protect and improve the soil's natural moisture retention capacity through numerous actions—reducing soil temperature swings, reducing maximal soil temperature reached in summer by shading the soil (a 20–40 degrees reduction in surface soil temperature is not uncommon!) and slowing evaporation of moisture in the top few inches of the soil.

As a side benefit, mulches help reduce summer and increase winter soil temperatures, encouraging greater soil food web activity higher up in the soil and reducing stress on plant root systems, while also increasing water and air storage capacity higher in the soil line. Mulch's temperature stabilizing properties are very helpful to growers who enjoy pushing zonal limits for their plantings, including perennials. For instance, softwood wood chip mulches have an R-value of around 1.5

per inch, hard woods half that, while straw is similar in R value to soft woods. Thus, a few inches of any such mulch significantly insulates the soil beneath and helps capture ground heat during cool periods and cools the plant roots during the strong sunny days of summer. This reduces plant stress, resulting in healthier plants and heftier yields.

In field trials on our farm, mulched soils, especially ones that used both an organic and living mulch, had soil temperatures 30 degrees lower than exposed soil.

Third, when used properly, mulches significantly reduce the need for weeding and the ability for seeds and other invasives to become established in your growing spaces. Depending on the type of mulch and other factors, mulches can reduce weed seed germination by as much as 90% by shading the soil and competing for soil resources with unwanted plants. Thus, they make an excellent upfront investment at the beginning of a growing season, saving countless hours of labor, feeding the soil food web over time, protecting the soil from compaction, and increasing water conservation and reducing the need to water.

Season shortening and organic mulches

One common concern and complaint with organic mulches, especially persistent ones like wood chips, is since they act as an insulator, they can hinder the ground from warming up quickly come late winter and early spring. This is a valid concern especially for market growers, who after a long winter may be low on finances and who may not be able to afford a multi-week delay in planting caused by heavy mulches coupled with a cool, wet spring. Thankfully, there are a number of possible solutions to this problem.

Some growers will rake back mulches come Spring in their growing spaces to expose the ground beneath for early season crops. Others will lay clear greenhouse plastic directly on the ground to capture solar gain and heat. Such hybrid methods—combining solarization and occultation which we discuss in other parts of the book—help extend your growing season and reduce weed load at the same time. Another method is to turn your growing spaces into year round, season extended low tunnels, caterpillar tunnels, or high tunnels that can be swapped between greenhouse plastic in the winter and shade cloth in the summer.

By keeping space in use year round, the ground never has an opportunity to get exceptionally cold, while come spring, the low tunnels' thermal gain more than offsets any loss caused by organic mulches. For beds that do not have low tunnels built over them, the same style of greenhouse plastic can be laid directly on areas of ground that need warmed first to similar effect, with the mulch either raked back or left in place.

Nature Knows Best: Organic Mulches

Of the many things that are worth a grower's praise, organic mulches are at the top of the list. Their benefits are almost too numerous to list, including:

Improving moisture and water retention

Organic mulches help store and retain water while also cooling the soil in summer, reducing evaporation and soil stress significantly. Such mulches protect the soil beneath from evaporation while storing and then slowly releasing their own moisture to the soil below. There are a few exceptions to this rule that we will discuss later.

Decreasing soil temperature

On a sunny July day in Kentucky, bare soil can reach over 100 degrees. Such heat causes rapid evaporation and moisture loss which has all sorts of deleterious and damaging effects on the soil beneath. The high temperatures cause significant stress to plants, especially shallow rooted varieties. They also drive the soil food web deep down into the soil, away from where some annual plant roots are found, decreasing plant nutrient and water uptake and increasing plant stress.

Organic mulches significantly reduce soil temperature by as much as ten to thirty degrees. This protects the plants and soil from all sorts of negative impacts that come with high temperatures. But note, this has a downside. Heavily mulched areas are slow to warm up in spring and also don't allow cold to penetrate as well in winter. This can result in increased pest populations and delayed planting if not managed properly.

Increasing biological activity of soil

Many beneficial soil dwellers, like worms, generally dislike light, heat, and dry conditions. Mulches raise the soil table not just in terms of moisture, which allows many soil creatures to work, but microbe and soil dweller activities by their shading and sheltering effect, and as noted above, moderating soil temperature, further contributing to their flourishing. In a sense mulches are micro terra-forming, creating a place much more conducive to the lives of these little laborers who comprise the soil food web. Organic mulches also provide a vital food source for a large swath of the soil food web, keeping particular parts and pieces of it well fed all year long.

Decreasing soil compaction and erosion

Mulches help spread out the weight of heavy objects—such as people, wheelbarrows, and even trucks and machinery—passing through growing spaces, minimizing or mitigating their negative impact on soil structure and reducing compaction. Mulches also protect soil from the force of erosion (wind and water) and degradation of soil caused by sunlight.

Increasing beneficial habitat

Snakes, toads, frogs, and all sorts of other beneficial critters and creatures love mulches (as do some pests as well!). Mulching well means encouraging the former while steps can be taken to reduce the populations of the latter.

Contributing to soil building

As they break down, living and organic mulches provide varied nutrition that feeds the soil food web and builds soil organic matter each season, often in a very rapid manner if used properly. They also protect the existing soil from organic matter loss through oxidation and other processes caused by exposure to sunlight and air. There is a reason forest floors in more temperate regions tend to have such fertile soil—the trees produce an annual and endless organic mulch that the forest floor enjoys coupled with an understory of other living vegetation that together rapidly assist soil accumulation.

Decreasing weed germination

One of the best parts of mulches is the reduction in weeds and weeding, along with the ease of weed removal compared to bare soil. Ever engage in a tug of war with a weed, only to rip off its head while its root system remained unharmed? Such days are generally a thing of the past with properly mulched soil.

A deep mulch blocks light and otherwise helps suppress weed seed germination and growth. Also, since most organic mulches are high carbon and low nitrogen, they help inhibit weed germination and growth at the soil horizon, where mulch meets soil, while not harming your garden plants.

Protect Plants From "Soil Splash"

Plastic, grass, wood, and living mulches protect plants from "soil splash." When rain hits bare ground, it can cause soil particles to bounce up into the air. The harder and heavier the rain, the more and higher the soil particles will go. These particles, now mixed with water, easily stick to the lower leaves on plants, spreading soil borne diseases. Thus, soil splash turns the blessing of rain into a disease ridden battlefield for your crops. Mulch stops soil splash before it starts.

Organic mulches include a wide array of options, from wood chips and straw to newspaper and leaves. Also, organic mulches and living mulches can work together synergistically, creating benefits that rapidly build and feed the soil from below and above at the at the same time. But not all growers are good with organic mulches.

Organic mulches

All organic mulches create a dark, moist and warm environment, ideal for fungi and pests to thrive. While some of these microorganisms and insects enhance the mulch by breaking it down causing it to release nutrients into the soil, others can cause harm by leaving behind toxic waste.

For some, politics and religion result in ruckus and rancorous debates. For growers, mulches seem to be the de facto divider. Peruse the internet and you will see long debates over what, where, when, how, and why to mulch, along with all sorts of comments about the pros and cons of mulching, especially with wood based mulches. So are organic mulches our deliverance or of the devil?

Devil or deliverer, what's the deal with organic mulches?

We use organic mulches extensively on our farm. In our view, the best way to settle a debate is to do field trials and see if other field trials and studies match up with our experience. In our field trials, we have discovered a lot of things about organic mulches and our particular climate.

Here are some observations from our field trials, various research studies, and other growers.

Climate: growers in warmer climates, especially ones that lack a true winter, tend to have more pest issues from organic mulches than those in cooler to cold climates, which tend to reduce pest populations dramatically through hard freezes. Solarization (see chapter 12) can play a key role in addressing this issue.

Chickens: growing spaces that give chickens or similar poultry access have lower pest populations than those that exclude pest predators. Well timed and managed chicken access has been shown to have a substantial beneficial effect on pest populations in a number of trials and studies. It also adds much needed nitrogen to help hasten the breakdown of larger chunks of material.

Chips vs. chaff: Wood chip mulches tend to encourage less pests and pest damage than straw mulches. They also tend to produce far larger yields.

7

Wood-Based Mulches

If the World were to end tomorrow, I would plant a tree today

—Martin Luther

Wood chips were one of the best performers in terms of moisture retention, temperature moderation, weed control, and sustainability.

—Linda Chalker-Scott, Ph.D., Puyallup Research and Extension Center

Few things are as amazing and available as trees. Therefore, the first and most common organic mulch family is made from them. Tree based mulches come in many shapes and sizes, along with trees themselves coming in many species. It is important to understand how to safely use these mulches. Misuse results in many damaged gardens and derailed growing operations every year.

First, we will cover tree based mulches without green matter: sawdust and wood shavings. Here we will also cover pure bark mulch. Then, we will cover mixed materials, wood chips, and ramial chipped wood. Last, we go green, discussing just the green material from trees: pine and leaf mulches. All of the above are commonly used on many farms and homesteads for animals, providing bedding, dust bathing, and contributing to compost making.

All only exist because of the beauty and ubiquity of trees. Thus, whenever possible, farms and homesteads should seek to preserve, protect, and improve not just growing spaces and pastures, but support areas such as forest and silvo-pasturage that provide the carbon necessary to build soil, bed animals, and bury weeds! It is difficult to grow your own straw, but growing trees and making your own chips is doable for many homesteaders and on many farms. PTO driven chippers for those with tractors or stand alone units are often available used and at very affordable prices.

Before we discuss the differences between each of the seven tree based mulches, I want to give an overview that applies to all tree based mulches and will help you use them safely and effectively.

Species of Tree

When it comes to mulch, not all trees are created equal for growing purposes and some are downright dangerous to a garden's produce. The main species to avoid is any of the walnut family—black walnut, butternut, hickories, and pecan—which contain a chemical called juglone, though black walnut contains the highest concentrations and is thus the most dangerous.

Cedar, eucalyptus, locust, and old growth redwood, which also contain a number of rot resistant chemicals, can be used, but generally require a longer aging process and if applied fresh to growing spaces, may hurt plants, hinder proper germination and pollination, harm soil food web activity, and hamper soil dweller action because of the repellant and antimicrobial effects of the volatile organics and other chemicals in the wood. So, these are best used for animal bedding (if they will not harm the animals you are bedding!) or otherwise aged first to break down the aromatic compounds before applying to growing spaces. Depending on the fineness of the chipping, usually two months is a safe time to wait before using them as mulch under composting conditions.

An easy way to check is to turn into a pile and smell—if the aroma is still aromatic, the chips need additional time to breakdown. Another sign is color—cedar (red) and locust (yellow) lose their color as they lose their aromatic and other compounds and break down. A final test for readiness? Fungus! If a pile of chips is growing fungi then it is ready for use as a mulch.

Some additional suspect species

The below species are okay to use, but need to be well rotted or well aged first.

Black cherry, camphor wood, cedar/juniper/yew, eucalyptus, osage orange, Pacific yew, pine/fir/spruce, red mulberry.

Walnut, locust, and old growth redwood need even more care and aging than the above. Another good rule of thumb is if it is colonized by fungus, mushrooms or mycelium, it should be garden safe.

Species will also dramatically affect speed of decomposition. In general, the softer the wood outside the conifer family, the faster the rate of decomposition. A grower can use this to their advantage, depending on the stage, current use, and future use of a particular space and what chips they have available species-wise. The setting that the chipper was set to will also impact speed of decomposition.

Note also, a grower's climate and then the climate conditions of each particular year will radically impact the speed of mulch decomposition, but especially wood mulches. Dry, arid growing regions will tend to have wood mulches behave far more persistently than moist climates. Windier and sunnier areas will tend, with sufficient moisture, to break down rapidly, especially on healthy soils.

A jog down juglone lane

Juglone is a chemical produced by any tree in the walnut family. The most common ones are black walnut, butternut, hickory, and pecan. It is prevalent in all parts of the tree, but especially the roots at all times of the year and the leaves during summer green peak. It is a tomato killer, though it may injure or inhibit the growth of numerous other plants.

Any spot on a property that once had a black walnut tree within up to eighty feet should be considered suspect for any plantings that juglone is known to harm. The roots, as the highest source of the chemical, are especially persistent and damaging if left in the ground after tree removal. Such a spot, without significant tillage and other tactics, will be a danger to such plants indefinitely until the root system is dealt with and removed.

For growers, the plants most sensitive to juglone include, but are not limited to:

- Solanaceous crops (tomatoes, potatoes, peppers and eggplant)
- Cabbages and some other species of crucifers
- Herbaceous perennials like asparagus, alfalfa, rhubarb, lilies.

There are a few ways to help break down juglone. Thermophilic (hot) composting has been shown in about thirty to forty days to degrade it until it is no longer detectable in the soil. Tillage as well will reduce its presence, though not nearly as effectively as proper composting. Thus, areas that have had walnut roots may require multiple passes and a few years before the soil will support contradicted plants.

Healthy, active soils also appear to help break down the chemical, as many soil critters enjoy a little juglone after a long day's work in the ground. Thus, a prudent grower can probably safely use walnut family based mulches if they are careful in their handling, allow proper aging and composting, and have healthy soils.

So, what if you have access to black walnut wood chips, sawdust, or wood shavings? These, I would suggest, should be used for animal bedding, especially for chickens, or for mixing into a multi-year hot compost system. The animal bedding can then be composted by combining with coffee grounds and other nitrogen and microbe rich materials. This finished compost can then, if used for garden, be worked in and the first year those areas can be planted to crops that are known to be unaffected by the presence of the chemical (carrots, corn, squashes, beans, and melons).

In the second year (and thus third year since the tree was chipped), I would be comfortable planting freely in such a space, knowing that little to no juglone should remain at this point.

- Winter—Walnut tree chipped
- Winter/Spring—Used for animal bedding in winter
- Summer—Composted
- Fall—Applied to growing space
- Spring—Grow safe crops
- Fall or spring following year—grow any desired crop

Factors That Affect Speed of Wood Breakdown

How long will wood chips last as a mulch or in a compost system? A number of factors are involved in their longevity.

Age of Tree: Older and harder wood varieties generally create a higher lignin, more persistent mulch than younger, softer wood trees.

Fineness of mulch: Mulch fineness follows an interesting curve. On the far ends (very fine, like sawdust or very coarse, like branches and large chips and chunks), decomposition is slower. As you approach the middle, small and medium sized wood chips, decomposition is faster. This is caused by the complex interplay of surface area, air, moisture, and compaction, and how all these impact the various forces that break down wood based mulches.

The greater the exposed surface area, the more quickly the wood will decompose up to a certain point, since the greater surface area allows more water, microbes, sunlight, weathering, and bugs to work on breaking down the wood. At some point, the particle size is so fine that the wood product tends to mat and compact, creating a mulch that actually has less, not more, surface area, water penetration, and air circulation. Here, decomposition is significantly slowed, since the main decomposers lack key resources necessary to break down the wood product, water and air. At the other end, large chunks, twigs, and sticks also have significantly less surface area, so their rate of decay is also decreased.

Age of material: Older is better, depending on your application. Fresh wood chips from foliage free winter felled hardwood trees will be quite persistent and slow to breakdown, having a carbon nitrogen ratio of as much as 800:1 along with other chemical compounds that are resistant to decay. These are a wonderful animal bedding and such a use will not only benefit the animals but significantly hasten their decomposition. These are also great for use in compost making or in growing space paths and other application.

Aged wood products (1–2 years old or older) will break down with great haste when applied to growing spaces. Indeed, after about twenty-four months, some aged wood chip piles start to become indistinguishable from soil depending on the species and amount of Ramial wood and leaf litter in the original mix. Thus, if you are especially in a hurry to create good soil, finding a supply of well aged wood chips can go a long way. Another option is to make chips from species of tree that have a higher nitrogen content—these include Black Locust, Mimosa, Alder, Redbud, Autumn Olive, Kentucky Coffee Tree, Golden Chain Tree, Acacia, and Mesquite, among many others.

Time of year harvested: During winter, when nature is quiescent (sleeping), trees can have a C/N ratio as high as 500:1. In summer, this ratio drops to as low as 200:1. Thus, wintertime wood chips are especially appropriate to first use as an animal bedding or in some other high nitrogen processing systems to capture excess nitrogen and odors. Summer chips once aged are a great direct mulch for growing spaces.

As a final note, **never** use a wood product derived from treated lumber. If you are not sure what you are getting is just true, pure wood, unadulterated wood, don't accept it or use it.

Microclimate of grower: As noted above, one often overlooked facet of using wood based mulches is how a grower's climate impacts their speed of decay. In general, moderately wet climates and regions with more moderate temperatures will break down wood based mulches fairly quickly. Too much or too little moisture will slow their decay, as will excessive heat or cold.

Cypress mulch

Fads come and go, but the environmental toll persists. Cypress mulch became popular because of its reputation, similar to cedar and locust, for containing chemicals that resisted rot and warded off pests. This caused a surge in popularity for cypress products, forcing makers to use younger and younger trees and overharvest existing groves. These immature trees contain far less if any of the natural chemicals that people are looking for when they purchase cypress mulches, while also harming sensitive environmental areas where the trees are common. Cypress groves are found mainly in low-lying coastal areas, thus serving as the first line of defense against storm surge and strong storm systems rolling in from the Gulf of Mexico. For this reason, conscientious growers will avoid using improperly harvested cypress mulches.

Termites and other trying pests

Many people express concern over creating pest problems, especially pests like termites that can do real damage to surrounding structures. First, the good news: the studies that have been done on the subject of termites and wood chips actually show wood chips are not an especially good environment for termites to thrive.

As long as you are not growing right against any buildings (and even then, as long as you leave a few inch gap), wood chip mulch produces no greater risks or problems than any other mulch.

Also, pest populations are one reason we encourage a one to two time a year annual "chickening" of your growing spaces, among other efforts to increase beneficial insect and predator populations. The best defense against garden pests is a good offense in and around the garden.

Third, for the issue of ants, something as simple as a borax sugar trap can easily take care of excess and aggressive ant populations that may be created or aided by heavy wood chip mulches in your growing spaces. It is also very easy to make.

1. Place one cup of water in saucepan and warm slightly.

2. Mix in 1/2 cup sugar and 3 tablespoons borax.

3. Soak up mixture with cotton balls or paper towels.

4. Place the towels or cotton balls in shallow dishes near where you see ants. We usually place them in nut butter or similar shallow jar lids.

5. Whatever you do, don't kill the ants you see! You want them to eat the cotton balls or paper towels and take it back to the nest, where the borax will disrupt the entire colony.

In our experience, within 2–5 days the above traps take out any problematic ant colonies. Note, if you are dealing with outdoor ants, the traps will need protection from the weather.

Sawdust

Sawdust is very fine wood particles, generally made by sawmills and woodworking operations. There is some debate over sawdust. Because of its very high surface area, it has the potential to absorb a large amount of water and break down quickly. In our experience, though, it also has an even stronger tendency to mat and compact, shedding rather than absorbing water and making an impermeable hard pan, especially when used to bed certain animals. It is not uncommon for people using sawdust to report multiple inches of rain not penetrating a multi-inch sawdust mulch. Since it creates an impermeable mat, the soil beneath may become anaerobic, causing other issues, including possible nitrogen loss.

We generally use sawdust only where we want a more persistent walkway, have an area that we want to significantly kill off invasive or persistent plants and sod, or as part of our animal bedding systems (we use a mixture of sawdust, coffee husks, COIR, straw, wood shavings, and wood chips for animal bedding), and then move that animal bedding mix to growing areas in the fall, giving it all winter to break down for spring planting. Sawdust mixed with wood shavings for chicken bedding applied to an area in the fall makes an amazing growing space come the following spring for many heavy feeders, including potatoes and corn.

Some growers have asked if sawdust is appropriate to use in paths. Generally, the reply is no. Heavy rain and other things can move sawdust from paths into growing beds, with deleterious results. Plants placed along the edges of beds will put roots out well into walkways, where sawdust can negatively impact their growth. Also, sawdust can release a number of problematic chemicals and compounds during decomposition, which then leach into the soil and surrounding beds. These and other factors make using sawdust near growing spaces a risk we don't recommend taking.

Wood Shavings

Wood shavings are incredibly similar to sawdust, so there is not much to add, save in mentioning their immense value as animal bedding, especially for young poultry like chickens and turkeys who tend to to eat sawdust, sometimes to their harm. Like sawdust, they are not appropriate for growing space use.

Wood shavings are available from many sources, but especially furniture makers. But that comes with a caveat/warning. Many furniture makers also work with laminates and treated lumbers, which gets mixed into their shavings and sawdust. These are not safe to use for garden or farm, animal or vegetable. So make sure any source is 100%

pure wood. This may require a collector to provide bags or a trash can or some other receptacle for this purpose. Such a small investment is worth the value of the shavings.

Barking up the Wrong Tree

Bark, the outer layer of a tree, is the final pure wood mulch option worth discussing. Bark differs from wood in many important ways. Consider the role of bark on a tree. It is meant to protect the tree from moisture loss and damage, like skin for people. Thus, bark contains suberin, a waxy substance that repels water, among many other differences between it and regular wood. This makes bark based mulches poor holders of moisture, especially until it has decomposed for six months to a year or longer, depending on species.

In some parts of the country, bark is processed with salt or held in areas that allow it to become highly weed and invasive species seed infested. Both of these are things to consider and watch out for if sourcing bark mulch. Chemically, bark is unlike wood chips (both heart and ramial). It is more resistant to decay than wood chips, most likely because of the high tannin and lignin content.

If all you can get is a more barky mulch, just be sure to source it carefully and realize that it generally takes a lot longer to break down than wood chip based mulches. Some places sell it in rather chunky pieces as well, further reducing its value. If you can source a thoroughly shredded bark mulch, it serves as an excellent persistent mulch, especially for paths and certain crop beds, and breaks down into excellent soil over time.

Wood Chips: Nature's Wonderful Wonder

Wood chips are one of our favorite homestead inputs. They are versatile, low to no cost, and easy to spread. In a study conducted in 1990, wood chips outperformed all the other mulches in water absorption (which provides slow release water to plants and helps cool surface soil), weed suppression (by hindering germination both through shading but also possibly by tying up nitrogen at the very edge of the soil surface, where many weed seeds find their homes), moderating soil temperatures, and soil moisture retention. They also scored highest in terms of overall sustainability.

Similarly, compared to other animal bedding options, wood chips also show superiority. One study showed that compared with straw, cow manure composted with wood chips retained 80% more nitrogen. In our experience raising chickens, pigs, and hogs, wood chips last longer, keep the animals cleaner as bedding, and create better finished compost. One place chips are not as good is for large animals needing some insulation in cold weather—here straw is superior. Also, with chickens and pigs, while we use predominantly wood chip mulch in loafing areas and coops, adding some straw and sawdust generally helps prevent compaction, caking and other problems. For animal bedding, diversity of materials appears to be king.

There are a number of places to get wood chips, often for free. If you are not too far from an urban area, contact local tree companies and offer your place as a drop spot. Many arborists have to pay or drive long distances to dispose of their loads, so as long as your location is not too inconvenient, they will often drop loads for free if you don't face too much competition. If you are a bit farther out, you may need to offer some cash, but a full dump truck load of wood chips goes a long, long way for a typical sized garden.

Another source is to contact the company responsible for trimming your local power lines. Sometimes this is a local company, sometimes it is a regional or national company. Each will have different protocols and practices for how an individual can request to be a drop site for chips. One thing to consider, especially if your area has a large amount of walnut or cedar and locust, is that the tree company will not be very keen on such exclusions, exceptions, and extra requests. They just want to dump the chips as easily and efficiently as possible. They don't get paid to go out of their way to get rid of the chips. If you are not certain what species are in the loads, make sure to follow the safe handling guidelines we have outlined in the book to protect both your garden and your animals.

Also realize, your access to wood chips may depend on your location. In some parts of the country, wood chips go directly to wood pellet stove fuel or similar manufacturers, especially in the northeast, and in some parts of the country, wood chips are not readily available because of the scarcity of trees or so much competitive pressure.

What would ya wood chip?

As noted above, a number of factors affect the rate of decomposition of wood

chips and wood products in general. A wise grower can use this to great advantage. For instance, major pathways would be a great place to put down a heavy layer of cardboard and then chip with wintertime fell, older, hardwood chips such as red or white oak. Such a pathway would then require minimal care and work for a number of years and provide a nice, clean, mud free access point to growing space for wheeling in additional materials or for workers.

On the other end, a bed that will need to be direct seeded especially with more tender, weaker plants come spring may benefit from well aged chips that will be substantially broken down after winter. If you are using certain planting tools, especially seed rollers, wood chips may not be appropriate for any beds that such tools will have to work with and in.

Also note, depending on how and from whom you are getting your chips, you may be able to exercise some control over their fineness. Modern mechanical chippers are adjustable for chip size. Medium sized chips from hard, winter wood make great animal bedding that then gets composted and applied to your growing spaces. Smaller chips are great aged for three to six months and then used as a weed suppressing mulch in growing spaces.

Depending on the size of chips, some growers will go through and hand pick out larger ones to use for kindling and fire starting.

A warning about pallet and waste wood

It appears that some places now sell mulch made from recycling old pallets and other waste woods from building demolition and construction. Such mulches may be made from treated lumber and other chemical laden or compromised wood. Thus, if you are purchasing mulch other than directly from a tree company that is only using trees, be very careful and make sure that the person knows exactly what they are offering and how it is made and what it contains. Getting the provenance and kind of wood and where it was sourced from in writing is not a bad idea depending on how much you are purchasing.

Sour wood chip power

One danger with wood based mulches is the possibility that they will turn "sour." If piled high, exposed to moisture, any compacted spots in the pile may turn anaerobic and start to ferment, creating large amounts of acetic acid inside the pile, along with methanol and ammonia gasses. Thus, before applying a wood based mulch to growing spaces, be sure to smell it. If it smells sour like vinegar or rotten eggs or has any other off odors, it needs aerated and rinsed by rain or hose before application. It will take a few weeks to a month before the mulch is suitable for any growing application.

Such chips if applied to a growing space with plants can do great damage to the plants and the soil. So if you have somehow managed to create a sour pile, make sure you turn and spread it, and allow nature to break down and wash away these chemicals before moving the chips into your growing spaces.

The height of chip piles drastically increases the likelihood of sour mulch. Piles over ten feet high are the most likely to develop this problem. So for both making and sourcing wood chip mulches, keep the piles under ten feet and turn them every so often.

Wood chips and water

One important caveat with wood chip mulches is how they relate to water. As one master gardener put it, a thick wood chip mulch primarily keeps water IN the soil. Such a mulch can in some climates or during extended dryer spells keep moisture OUT as well, by absorbing small amounts of rainfall or irrigation and keeping it from reaching the soil below.

When plants are first put out, the above needs to be considered, as do plant needs during dryer periods. Checking the soil underneath a mulch is an easy way to assess soil moisture status and watering needs. With wood chip mulches and mulches in general, drip tape or light flood style irrigation works far better than air (sprinkler style) water applications. It is better to focus adding water to the soil in a larger amount in a smaller area than by scattering it all over, where it merely sits and absorbs into the significant wood chip barrier. Depending on your growing space, a swale, raised bed system allows for easy occasional flood irrigation into the swales, which then slowly feed water directly into the soil of the adjoining raised bed.

For our farm, when needed, we will place hoses at key areas of the garden and allow them to run for 10–20 minutes to thoroughly irrigate the soil underneath the mulch. Since our growing space is on a slight slope on a hill, the water naturally runs and spreads across the landscape, easily penetrating underneath the mulch for maximum effect and water conservation.

Why wood you hurt your plants?

Many growers have been told that wood based mulches will tie up soil nitrogen, stunting or stopping plant growth. Also, a number of sources claim wood has no nutritional value. Both of these qualify as good ole fashioned misinformation. Let's deal with each in turn.

It is correct that fresh wood products tilled into soil will cause a significant drop in available soil nitrogen levels, to the point of often rendering soil unable to grow most anything. This is why tilling in large amounts of wood chips is not recommended. But when wood chips and wood based mulches, except sawdust and wood shavings, are piled on top of healthy soil, they pose minimal threat to plantings. The only nitrogen they can tie up is where the wood surface and soil surface meet. This is nowhere close to where most seeds or transplants are drawing nutrition, including nitrogen. After many years of using wood chips, we have never seen them adversely affect direct seeding or transplanting that was done properly.

Now, if all a grower does is constantly coat their garden or growing spaces in wood chips, neglecting compost, cover cropping, and all the other activities that create healthy soil, they will create problems, including nitrogen problems. But this isn't caused by the wood chips—it is caused by the gardener and their neglect of good growing principles! Wood chips are not some magic cure-all for everything a growing space needs. Also, a diet of only wood chips will alter the soil food webs balance in favor of perennial plants, which is another reason why some people run into issues after many years of relying on wood chip mulches as their main approach to building healthy soil. As long as you use well made compost, cover crops, companion planting, and other techniques that benefit the soil, there is no risk to also using large amounts of wood chips.

Second, a number of sources make the rather baffling claim that wood contains no nutrient value, while they also praise wood ash as a great source of various minerals and other compounds for the garden. Unless they believe in some sort of alchemy, such a claim runs into the rather small hurdle—wood ash is acknowledged to be loaded with nutrients and could not contain anything that wasn't present in the original tree. We also have other studies that show trees contain all sorts of minerals and other nutrients. Trees are so nutritious that we use them as a food stuff, tapping their sap to make all sorts of delicious syrups such as maple.

Wood chips do have a highly variable nutrient profile—species of tree, age, and where on the tree chips are sourced from all impact final nutrient profile. For the most part, wood chips' contribution to your soil's nutrient profile will be modest, unless you are using wood chips made mostly or exclusively from the young, fresh growth on the tree when in green. These chips, known as Ramial Chipped Wood (RCW), are what we turn our attention to next.

Ramial Chipped Wood (RCW)

While Ramial chipped wood is just another form of wood, it is a special form and deserves special mention. Ramial chipped wood differs from wood chips in general in that it is only derived from the young, soft growth of trees, generally deciduous varieties. This growth tends to be about 3 inches and under in diameter. It has a much lower C/N ratio and the young wood is far less fibrous and has a very different composition than older growth wood. Also, it contains significantly more nutrition than any other part of the tree. These young branches are where all the real growth and life of the tree is taking place. Up to 75% of all the nutrients in a tree can be found in the ramial wood.

This better carbon/nitrogen ratio coupled with the change in physical structure of RCW creates a soil builder that breaks down with exceptional speed. Unlike regular wood chips, which can take two to five years to fully cycle into soil, RCW will usually completely break down in a single growing season. Three to six months is the expected life span.

Thus, RCW is used very differently than most wood mulches.

RCW is available commercially in some parts of the country. It is also relatively easy to make on a small scale, requiring nothing more than a wood chipper, trees, and time. RCW is especially helpful for humification (the process of organic matter being degraded into humus).

Unlike other wood mulches, RCW is not as effective as a weed suppressor, since it does not tie up nitrogen at the soil horizon like higher carbon wood mulches. Thus, if weed suppression is a high priority, a greater thickness of RCW is needed or a mixed mulched is advised—RCW applied first, followed by a second, more suppressive mulch on top. This has the added benefit of sometimes helping hasten the RCW's decomposition, since the lower level retains more moisture.

The biggest drawback to RCW is the labor and cost involved to produce it. Unlike loads of wood chips (which are accessible in many parts of the country for free or for low cost), RCW should be made from branches no larger than three inches (7cm) in size. Thus, it is primarily made from pruning deciduous trees and then shredding them or chipping them. Such pruning is slow and labor intensive, especially compared to taking down an entire tree, as is the chipping process. A half day of work may yield only a hundred or so gallons of RCW. For those with orchards or other situations that require such pruning, you can recoup some of the cost in terms of time and labor by making all that material into RCW rather than having to otherwise dispose of it by burning or some other method.

Some companies specialize in pruning work and thus may have a larger volume of RCW that a grower can lay claim to and get a hold of. Often, when dealing with tree companies that trim power lines, loads of wood chips will be laced with veins of "black gold" that forms after just a month or so of aging—these veins are RCW.

Coppicing and Pollarding

One interesting set of techniques for generating large amounts of small diameter work is coppicing (from the French word to cut) and pollarding (from the word pole or head). Many species of trees will naturally regenerate from the root system and base once cut down. Some species (low sap deciduous like oak) are especially appropriate and apt for this technique. The regeneration can be quite prolific, with the new growth reaching two or more meters per year. This is because it enjoys the benefits of a fully established root system to support a much smaller plant. Instead of energy going into maintaining a large established tree, it can be focused into the regrowth.

Coppicing and pollarding both take advantage of this attribute, with a single difference—coppicing is done at ground level, while pollarding is done at chest level or higher. Practically, both techniques have many benefits, including keeping trees from interfering with power or sewer/septic lines.

Both techniques can be used to provide a steady source of smaller diameter firewood or wood for making biochar or RCW from. Such smaller wood would also allow you to efficiently and affordably make wood chips for mulch using a PTO or gas powered three to six inch chipper.

Don't Get Conned: Conifers and RCW

Trees can be classified in many ways. One of the main divisions is between deciduous and conifers, also known as evergreens. Conifers are known for producing their seeds in cones, having leaves in the shape of needles or small, flat scales, and having a much more triangular, upward shape to their growth.

In colder climates, RCW produced from conifers can pose significant problems to soil development. Conifers contain particular chemicals that inhibit soil formation and RCW break down—primarily polyphenols, tannins, and turpenes. These chemicals are why pine trees are used to create products like Pine-Sol and turpentine. Thus, their use in RCW should be strongly limited, especially the further north one resides. In tropical climates, these chemicals pose less of problem as the soil activity is so high that soil organisms digest them speedily, but in cold climates they can hinder soil formation and harm the soil food web.

This makes sense, as most old growth conifer forests have little other vegetation or deciduous trees mixed in among the conifers. The above chemicals confer upon conifers a competitive advantage in establishing themselves in a range and outcompeting and protecting themselves from succession by other species.

Wood Mulches and the Soil Food Web

Different growing spaces prefer different soil balances between fungi and bacteria. A forest, for instance, generally has a soil with a ratio of a hundred fungi for each bacteria. A pasture's ratio will be around one to one. Annual growing spaces tend to have more bacteria than fungi.

Some writers have raised concerns about growers using woods chips season after season as a mulch in annual growing spaces. Over time, this can increase fungal populations, upsetting the balance between bacteria and fungi in the soil that annuals prefer. Decomposing wood primarily contains compounds like lignin and cellulose that are too large and complex for bacteria to break down, but are the favorite foods of fungi. Thus, fungi will proliferate while bacteria will diminish in heavily wooded areas, which is why old growth forests have soil populations dominated by fungi with few bacteria to go around.

This is a valid concern, but mainly to growers who are not utilizing a multifaceted approach to soil building and maintenance. If all a grower does is throw wood chips on the garden, then yes, over time, the soil will become unbalanced and overrun with fungi. But, when cover cropping, worm castings, composting, animal manures and other such tools are deployed along with wood chips or wood based mulches, there is little risk of creating a systemic imbalance in the soil's micro-ecology and microbiology. These other methods help keep in check the soil fungal populations while bolstering and feeding the bacterial side, ensuring the soil remains vibrant and healthy for a wide variety and range of crops.

For concerned growers, and as a general maintenance recommendation, when getting annual or biannual soil tests, the soil food web should also be tested. If after a few years of testing the balance appears to be stable and healthy, testing can then be done every other to every three years unless the grower deems it necessary to keep a closer eye on what is happening. Also, a grower in different climates who has enough area in production can experiment and compare how different applications and soil stewardships approaches affect the soil not just nutritionally, but microbiologically.

Spreading the Wealth: Efficiently Moving and Applying Mulches

For larger growing spaces, there are three indispensable tools to make mulching manageable. The first is a two wheeled wheelbarrow. Single wheeled versions, while less expensive, reduce the amount of material someone can move by over half while increasing the amount of work to move that half load by a factor of two or more. So, it is basically four times more work or more for moving the same amount of mulch. A two wheeled version by distributing the weight across two places requires far less upper body strength and causes far less fatigue since the one moving the wheelbarrow doesn't have to do all the work balancing the contents. The difference in moving and spreading a dump truck load of wood chips is significant.

If you have the money, another option that we have found to be superior even to a two-wheel wheelbarrow is a garden cart. Now that we have a garden cart, we didn't even bother to replace our wheelbarrow when it broke. Instead, we are going to get a second garden cart! For moving just about anything, a high quality garden cart is quite possibly the next best thing to a tractor. Even our kids who are under 10 can move loads of wood chips, firewood, and other heavy materials when they have four wheels helping.

Second and third, a good pitchfork and shovel. The best I have found—and yet they cost only a bit more than the ones sold at the big box stores—are made in Germany by SHW. Such tools are generally not available at chain stores. Some local, specialty garden and growing businesses will offer them, and they can also be acquired online by supporting such businesses like Earth Tools. Your arms, back, legs, husband, wife, and great grandchildren will all thank you for the investment in good tools that may well find their way into their hands one day.

Leaf Mold/Mulch

The final tree based mulch involves the use of leaves, especially leaves that come off the trees in the fall. Tree leaves vary in terms of their carbon/nitrogen ratio significantly (by a factor of six from bottom to top). Also, some types of leaves (generally hardwood) are very low in calcium. This slows their decomposition significantly. If you are using a lot of such leaves, adding some calcium can help hasten their breakdown.

Depending on a grower's location, leaf mulch may be relatively easy and free to access. Many areas of the country offer residents leaf collection in the fall. This is one of the biggest benefits of leaves as a mulch of soil amendment. Such places may offer this material free to growers who have the ability to haul it away.

Leaf mulch is best made by shredding the leaves first, though, adding a labor and machinery intensive step. Without shredding, leaves are easily blown around by wind and weather. A good leaf mulch made from shredded or composted leaves is about 3–6 inches deep. As the leaves decompose, the mulch will settle to 1–3 inches.

Some growers will use floating row cover to keep leaves in place until rain and decomposition has stabilized the mulch in place, especially over beds of garlic or similar crops.

Don't Rake 'Em!

Leaves fall at the worst time of year for keeping them seed free. Just as everything is working hard to drop its final seed load before winter, leaves come toppling off the trees into lawns and yards below. In city lots, which tend to be well mowed, seed contamination risk is real, but somewhat low. But collecting leaves out in the countryside, where lawns often go over long between mowing, increases the risk substantially.

If you want to collect seed free leaves without having to stay on top of mowing, using a large tarp of some kind set below a treeline is an exceptionally efficient way to do so. Each year, we spread a few tarps along wood edge. Once full, we empty the tarp into a few large trash cans, smashing down and breaking up the leaves some in the process. Then we easily roll the cans to the appropriate location, either garden for mulch or barn for worm food.

Pine Straw

Another green material option for mulch comes from our friends the conifers, pine straw. Pine straw is collected from pine or similar evergreens, dried, and then bundled to sell as mulch. Unlike wood chips, which some growers can source for free or low cost, generally pine straw is going to require some cash. Unlike wood chip and some other mulches, pine straw is much easier to spread and a single bundle provides fairly good coverage for the price. It is also more persistent than many other mulches, making it an attractive choice for beds that are in perennials or transplants like sweet potatoes and similar crops.

Pine needles have a very slight acidifying impact on soil over time. But studies have shown that this is so mild as to be of no concern at all.

8

Grass-Based Mulches

In some areas, wood based mulches are hard to come by, but grass based mulches—straw, hay, and grass clippings—are abundant most everywhere. In this chapter, we will explore these particular mulches. They have many of the same benefits of wood based mulches, but they break down far more rapidly. They all help retain moisture, moderate soil temperatures, and feed the soil food web while providing fertility and building soil organic matter, among other benefits. It just tends to take more of them to achieve the same weed suppression as wood chip mulches or contribute as much organic matter to the soil.

But unlike wood based mulches, these have a number of significant risks to your growing spaces. Risk that if not handled rightly can derail your growing for many, many years to come.

Summary

- Straw and hay are common alternatives to wood chip mulches.
- Straw is generally more durable a mulch, while hay is more enriching to the soil.
- Both carry the risk of unwanted and highly damaging herbicide contamination.
- Hay generally also carries far more weed seed risk, especially for difficult to deal with, unwanted species of grasses and weeds. Some hays are much lower in weed seed risk and load (like alfalfas).

- Straw and hay may also increase certain pest pressures, especially rodents, though straw tends to contribute to this problem more than hay. We have found that using either old straw (spread and allow it to break down over winter for spring use or from a previous year's bales that have weathered) or shredded straw provides better weed suppression and less pest pressure than fresh, whole straw.

Straw and Hay

Straw is the stalks and stubble left over from growing various grains. Unlike hay, it is relatively seed free if produced properly and higher in carbon while lower in moisture, nitrogen, and other nutrients. Straw, like most other mulches, is often also used for animal bedding. Over the past decade, it has also become very popular as a straight growing medium, either as whole bales which are amended and then planted directly into, or as a mulch.

Hay is generally mixed species of pasture plants, cut, dried, and then baled for animal food. Unlike straw, that has large diameter pieces and a more brown/yellow appearance, hay is greenish brown in tint, with at times a slightly sweet scent. Sometimes, hay is more particular plant-wise, such as alfalfa or clover hay, though it is rare to have a 100% pure hay. Hay, unlike straw, will generally have large amounts of grass and weed seed. This is why farmers will often use it to fix damaged areas of pasture by spreading bales on the ground for the animals to eat in place. The leftover seed and material, accompanied by the fresh animal manure, helps to quickly restore a degraded or damaged patch of pasture.

Hay tends to have higher fertility value than straw, especially for nitrogen, but often for almost all other nutrients as well. It has a much lower carbon to nitrogen ratio, so it breaks down more quickly. Both carry the risk of herbicide contamination.

Which has a greater risk is subject to debate—I treat both as guilty until proven innocent. You should treat both (along with compost, animal manures, and any other similar inputs) with the utmost seriousness since the cost of using contaminated straw or hay is quite high. At the end of this chapter, we will have an entire section discussing herbicide contamination in inputs and how to protect your growing spaces from it. But for now, let's look at some of the practicals of these mulches.

Round versus Square Bales

Straw and hay are generally available in two forms, standard square bales and large round bales. Round bales are generally *sixty to eighty percent less expensive than square bales* for the same amount of material. That trade off comes at a cost—they require a good deal more strength, a small crew, or a tractor or skid steer to move. A small pickup truck can handle a single round bale, which in my area run about 600–900 pounds. A larger, heavy duty truck can handle two if loaded properly. A truck and small trailer will let you move four to six or more bales, depending on the truck and trailer. Just make sure both the truck and trailer have the power and weight rating for the amount you are trying to haul.

In many areas, if you are getting a large amount of either, farmers will deliver, sometimes for free, especially if you time your order well. If they have to move straw or hay from a satellite location back to the main farm or a storage location, they would just as soon bring it directly to you and save the extra labor, storage space, and time. So try to plan your purchasing accordingly.

Round bales also have the advantage of being able to be rolled out like a carpet, allowing a single person to quickly cover large areas once a bale is positioned. Square bales have the advantage of being easier for a single person to handle, along with being easier to stack and store. They also are great for making raised beds, hot boxes and frames, composting piles, and a host of other things. Having some of both types of bales is not a bad idea if you have space and access to both sizes.

Both types require proper storage, though square are generally easier to store than round. You will rarely see square bales left out in fields or under tree lines in my area, but you will see round bales left exposed on almost every road and field. This is one concern with round bales, especially hay and to a lesser extent straw. They degrade rapidly when left out in the weather, especially wet weather, and especially when left sitting in direct contact with the ground and exposed to the sun after curing. If you are purchasing bales from someone who doesn't store them properly, get them as soon as possible and get them into proper storage as soon as possible as well. If you are purchasing older, weathered, or rotten bales, these should come at a discount over the normal going rate. Also, don't store old, rotted bales near good quality bales! Let them stay outside close to where you plan to use them.

Storing Straw and Hay

Unlike wood chips, straw and hay require special storage. While wood chip mulches benefit from aging out in sun and weather, straw and hay do not. Indeed, improper handling of hay creates a dangerous fire risk. It should be in a place sheltered from rain and raised up off the ground to protect it from moisture, similar to firewood.

The first part is the expensive one—finding space in a barn, shed, or lean-to to store your straw and hay. Another option is to purchase some kind of heavy duty tarping, or get your hands on an old, good condition silage tarp. In my experience, both standard store-bought tarps and the vinyl billboard tarps do not hold up well enough for protecting hay and straw (or firewood). As a temporary measure, they are acceptable, but over the course of a winter in my area they tend to degrade too quickly and let too much moisture and water through. While it seems expensive to store hay and straw in a barn or similar structure, when you consider the cost (both money and time wise) of putting up straw and hay, it is a steal. Improperly stored straw and hay lose up to 30% of their volume and significant amounts of their nutrition. Moldy and weathered sections don't spread as well as mulch, either.

The second part—raising the bales off the ground, is the inexpensive side of storage. The easiest way to do this is often free—find used pallets to stack the bales on. This works for both square and round bales. If you absolutely can't get pallets, you can make rails using pieces of wood or even small diameter (4 to 6 or so inch) tree limbs. Another great option in my area is the seconds of cedar or similar 4x4s from the local sawmill. These are especially good for round bales, where three runners is warranted, especially if double stacking height wise, because of the greater weight. The third runner helps ensure the bales don't sag in the middle, creating ground contact and inhibiting air flow around the bales.

Note that round bales are harder to loft and their shape doesn't allow them to pack together as tightly as square bales, so they generally take up more space for the same amount of material. Without equipment, it is almost impossible to do multiple levels like with square bales and take advantage of them stacking together more tightly. My kids and I can stack square bales 15 feet high in our barn by ourselves, with no equipment, not even a ladder. The bales themselves if you stack them right make an easy way up and down. We have yet to find a way to get a single round bale up on the others apart from heavy equipment.

When sourcing hay, make sure the farmer properly harvested, baled, and dried the bales before you bring them in and stack them in a structure. Hay fires take out countless barns and other buildings each year across the United States. Also make sure to keep an eye on the bales for the first few weeks in case any start to heat up and need removed and even spread out to stop the risk of a fire. There are now bale thermometers you can purchase for this purpose. If you are handling a lot of hay, it is well worth having one on hand.

Straw, Hay and Seeds

One other concern with straw is residual seeds. It is important that the straw be relatively seed free, or the means of weed suppression becomes the means of their expansion. Sometimes this happens because either an ill-informed store salesperson or otherwise ill-informed individual is selling hay as straw (don't laugh, I have seen it happen first hand!). Generally speaking, a grower should be able to tell the difference between hay and straw by sight and smell. Hay tends to smell sweet, have smaller and slimmer stalks, and have clover and other crops mixed in that you can identify by the stem and leaf structures of the stuff that makes up the bale. Straw is coarser and more earthy in smell, has thicker and woodier stalks that are yellow to golden brown in shade, and should show little to nothing else mixed in. Hay generally is less uniform in appearance than straw.

There are a few ways to deal with any remaining grain seed in straw prior to use. By setting out the bales and allowing them to become rained on a few weeks prior to spreading as mulch, a grower can cause seeds to germinate and then hopefully die back before use. This lightens the seed load significantly. It does make the bales significantly heavier to handle, so we stack right where we plan to spread them. This also helps the straw stay in place better when we spread, since fresh straw tends to not stay in place if there is any kind of wind. If using it, it sometimes helps to apply it right before rain or to water it lightly to help it settle.

Straw and Hay vs. Wood Chips

Straw and hay differ from wood chips significantly. For this section, to simplify things, I am just going to refer to straw, but everything I say applies equally to hay. First, it takes far more straw to achieve the same weed suppression effect as wood chips, since sunlight penetrates straw more easily and straw does not tie up nitrogen at the mulch-meets-earth horizon like wood based mulches. Whereas two to three inches of wood chips are all that is needed to substantially suppress weeds, six or more inches of straw are required for the same suppression. Both methods make the removal of any weeds significantly easier, since both help keep soil moist and uncompacted.

Chopping straw either by using a lawnmower or a tree chipper can increase straw's weed suppression and insulative properties, while also making it easier to spread and less likely to blow around and away. Wind is another issue with straw, which unlike wood chips, can easily become airborne, especially for the first week or so after application until the straw moistens, settles, and mildly compacts. If you are in a windy location, chopping straw, spreading, and then immediately watering it down is a must to keep the straw in its wanted spot.

Straw's main benefit over wood chips is that it is easier to spread and breaks down into soil more quickly. Two people can straw a significant area in short order if they are strong enough to carry full sized straw bales or roll out round bales. Each square bale will cover about 80–100 square feet. If your square bales are around 60 pounds, an average round bale (in my area 800 pounds) is equivalent to about 14 square bales. Given that a round bale is $25–40 dollars and square bales are $4–5, you see the opportunity for significant savings. For fifty dollars I can get two round bales—the equivalent of 28 square bales—or 10 square bales. It is like getting almost 3 times as much for free, not to mention the labor savings that round bales offer when rolling them out compared to having to hand spread square bales. The only caveat is if the round bales were stored outside—it is still a better deal, but the bales may have lost some of their volume and quality to weathering.

Kids can get in on the action after the bales have been broken open by doing the actual spreading, and generally kids do it with a great deal of vigor and enjoyment. Straw will typically not last beyond six months, so its contribution to soil building will be smaller but realized sooner than wood based mulches. Straw tends to attract earthworms and other soil decomposers and microorganisms just like wood mulches. But straw also tends to feed the soil food web in a more balanced fashion, keeping fungal and bacterial populations more balanced than wood chip based mulches will.

Straw, in our experience, also tends to attract particular pest issues when used as a mulch. If you manage your growing spaces well, this may self-correct over time as beneficial predator species move in to eat the various bugs that like to live in the straw. Just realize that for the first few growing cycles, you may see additional pest pressure, especially from squash bugs.

Another approach we have taken to cut down on straw's pest promoting tendencies is to apply it in the late fall or early winter, allowing it to decompose and settle down before spring planting. This reduces the amount of air space while not compromising its weed suppression. Also, the straw will be nicely stuck in place come spring. This method does have some drawbacks, though. First, since it insulates the ground, in a mild winter or climate it can increase some pest pressure by protecting them over winter since the soil will not get as cold. Second, since the straw is already broken down, unless you applied a very heavy layer in the late fall, it may not suppress weeds as well or as long next season.

A House Made of Straw and Hay

One major concern with straw is its attraction of larger pests, especially of the rodent family—mice, squirrels, rats, voles, and moles, among others. Both grass and wood mulches can serve as wintering grounds for slugs and other smaller species of pests. This issue will be exacerbated for growers in warmer climates or for all growers after shorter, milder winters. Growers who already struggle with certain pest populations like the above may want to avoid straw completely until the pests are under control, lest they provide the perfect population protection program to said pests.

Indeed, this is one of the reasons we use far less straw than wood chips. For growers that use significant and consistent straw mulching, integrated pest management practices are a must. Chickens, ducks, turkeys, and similar animals are crucial to removing pests at certain points of the growing cycle. Cats or similar predators like certain breeds of dogs are crucial to chasing off and catching those from the rodent family. Traps and other measure may also be necessary. Some growers get away with continuous straw mulches by incorporating tillage at the beginning of every season. Since we avoid tillage, such a system is not an option for us. But for those who can use tillage responsibly, it serves as another means to reduce pest pressures in a heavily straw based system.

In field trials we have seen superior results with wood based mulches compared to hay. For instance, we planted a number of wood chipped versus straw potato beds. Not only did the wood chip beds outyield the straw beds substantially (at about 30% more yield per bed), but the potatoes in the wood chipped bed showed almost no insect or other damage. Over half the potatoes planted in straw showed various forms of pest damage. It is good to note, the straw was not chopped or aged/applied in the late fall/early winter, and thus experimenting with wood chips, straw, and chopped straw would be a helpful comparison. Many growers I spoke to have had excellent results with straw and hay mulches, especially for non-root crops.

Using Chickens to Deseed Straw

While straw should be relatively seed free, sometimes that isn't the case. My potatoes this spring are inundated with wheat grass, the gift of a large amount of wheat straw we used to protect them from frost that was clearly insufficiently threshed!

Depending on your setup, chickens are an efficient way to deseed leftover grains from straw. After spreading the bales, give the chickens access to the space for a few days, and they will generally remove the majority of any remaining seedheads. Then deny them access and go back to planting. Remember, if you are selling produce, this is not acceptable under food safety rules unless the time between the chicken crew and your produce planting and harvesting meets the minimum withdrawals. It is a great way to get free chicken feed though!

Pre-fertilizing Straw Before Spreading

Another approach to straw involves allowing chickens or rabbits to "pre-fertilize" it by using it as bedding. This material can then be spread in the late fall or early winter over growing spaces. Suggested rates are about 8–24 inches deep, depending on how compacted the material is to start with. It will rot down nicely, while also enriching the soil and reducing the need for any additional fertilizers. Producing this amount of material may or may not be an option for every grower, but for certain crops this could provide an excellent way to deal with both weeds and soil fertility at the same time each fall in preparation for spring planting.

Hay Mulch and the Weed Seed Treadmill

Ruth Stott originally popularized using hay as a mulch for garden plants. The first time I read about it, I wondered, "What about the weeds?" Weeds are something we take very seriously on our farm. We have a number of species, including some dual reproducers (by both seed and rhizome) that have taken years to get under control in our growing spaces. Many are literally a pain to deal with—pigweed and thistle and a few others that fight back when you try to remove them.

With hay, some growers report that it results in the "hay mulch treadmill." Once you get on, you can't get off, or the built up bank of grass and weed seeds explodes back to life. If you do decide to move from hay to other mulches, solarization or similar techniques are a must to reduce the built up seed bank. During the growing season, hay mulch must remain deep enough to thoroughly suppress weeds or you will easily be overwhelmed by the innumerable weeds waiting for the right opportunity to spring back to life in your growing space.

Grass Clipping Mulch

I almost didn't include this mulching option, since it strikes me as both impractical and overly risky. After it came up a few times at conferences and in consulting, it became clear that I needed to mention it. Grass clippings are the trimmings from lawns and similar locations. They are not a mulch I use nor recommend, for a few reasons. Let's go through why.

1. They can easily contain grass-seed.

This is the primary reason I don't use grass clippings. Most people don't realize that long before the seed heads of grass push out of the stalks of the plant, the lower stems may contain viable seed. Given that a single plant can produce hundreds, if not thousands, of seeds, a small mistake in terms of timing, weather, or whatever can result in an exponential undoing of all your previous years of weeding.

I have invested far too much time and energy ridding my growing spaces of weeds to run the risk of a massive increase over a low quality mulch like clippings. This alone is enough for me, but if you need more convincing:

2. They can cause soil imbalances

Grass clippings are high in phosphorus and thus, over time, especially if you are applying compost and animal manures, can push your soil out of balance very easily. For most growers, grass clippings are an unneeded source of fertility. A number of times I found that a grower's soil imbalances could be traced back to repeated applications of grass clippings coupled with animal manure based composts.

3. You are robbing Peter to pay Paul

Your lawn and other areas need nutrition, organic matter, and care just as much as your garden. By taking grass clippings and moving them into your garden, you are degrading your grasslands, lawn included. Over time, you are going to create issues if you continue to relocate your lawn's already more limited fertility loop.

4. They can contain herbicide and other chemical residues

Especially if you are getting lawn clippings from public spaces, city collection sites, or standard lawn care operations, you run the risk of getting batches contaminated with herbicides and other lawn chemicals. Each year, many of my friends have come home to their lawns having been accidentally treated by lawn care companies (what an oxymoron!). This should give you an idea how widespread herbicide applications are in many large cities.

Between the herbicide and weed seed risks, I can't recommend using grass clippings. For the amount of time and labor needed to produce even at a small volume yourself, you can bring in far greater amounts of mulch that is better for your soil and less risky as well. So, now you have my thoughts on grass clippings as a mulch and soil amendment. Feel free to disagree, but if you run into one of the above issues, don't say I didn't warn you!

Herbicide Contamination: The Gift That Keeps on Giving

All three grass based mulches have a shared risk—herbicide contamination. This is an issue that every grower should take very seriously. Herbicide contamination has always been a danger, but the last ten years have seen a shift that has increased this risk to unimaginable proportions. Some herbicides no longer impact just a single crop or even a season of crops. Rather, multiple years of production can be lost if a grower makes a mistake and exposes their growing space to some of these new formulations.

As herbicide resistance spread in the early 2000s, chemical companies began to develop new formulations, both as ready replacements for when glyphosate and other formulas failed and for other applications where total burn down was desired. Some of the new formulations were just combination herbicides—2,4 D plus picloram (known as Grazon). These are terrible if you get them into your growing spaces, but not fatal. You will probably lose a year or so of growing, but then be back in business. Do note though if you carry any certifications (organic, certified naturally grown, or the like), those may take years to regain, even if your growing is only impacted for a season or so.

But others were something new, the pyralids. Specifically aminopyralid and clopyralid. Both make other herbicides look like a slice of heaven, but the first is far worse. At just one part per billion, all that grows well is corn and other grass if this stuff gets into your soil. With a half life of three to five years, it sticks around in the soil for a very long time, especially if you start with even moderate concentrations. Also, unlike other herbicides, these are unaffected by composting, animal consumption, or other common methods of remediation. Even better, currently there is no easy test for if any of the common vectors contain the herbicide. Careful sourcing is your only and best defense, along with bio-assays for composts and other inputs you bring on farm.

Thus, straw is one of the soil inputs I would urge growers to be fastidious about in their sourcing. Grains are one of the most heavily sprayed crops and often enjoy the worst of the worst kinds of chemicals: glyphosate, 2-4 D, fungicides, and synthetic fertilizers. Some of these chemicals can take a very long time to break down. So, with every bale of straw, you expose your garden, animals, and thus the food that eventually enters your body, to a steady stream of dangerous chemicals and the constituents they create as they break down. These have been shown to accumulate in the soil, harming the soil food web and the health of your plants, while contributing to the formation of superweeds and superpests, and are also implicated in development of many modern diseases. We want to neither import nor support these growing methods or growers if at all possible.

Even if it takes some time and costs more up front, truly clean straw is worth securing. In our area, when clean straw is available (we primarily get native Kentucky wild grasses, switchgrass, and other such species from a 5,000 acre tract of land in conservation easement), we stock up, since straw doesn't go bad when stored properly. It takes up one whole bay of our barn (a 10x8 by 14 foot tall area), but we count that as space and money well spent. A full bay (150–200 bales) will last us about two years between animal bedding, laying boxes, mulching, and other miscellaneous applications.

Some crops, such as oats and rye, are less likely to be sprayed.

Herbicide Trade Names

Common Name	Trade Name
picloram	Tordon, Grazon
triclopyr	Garlon, Remedy
clopyralid	Stinger, Transline, Hornet
aminopyralid	Milestone, Forefront

How to Do a Bioassay

If you are bringing composts of any kind onto your place, one way to test them for possible herbicide contamination is to do a bioassay. It is a simple way to see if there is anything detrimental to your plants in the product.

Start with high quality, fast germinating and growing seeds, like bush bean. Make two trays using the exact same seeds, generally of 12–24 plants each. In one tray, use a standard potting or seed starting mix. In the other, use a mix that incorporates some of the compost you are looking to purchase. Generally, compost is used at a rate of about 10–20% of the mixture. Plant, water, and care for the seedlings as you usually would. Compare results over the coming three to four weeks. Look for common signs of herbicide contamination—leaf curl, discoloration, poor germination, and the like. If both trays perform poorly, you will need to do the experiment over, as the seeds you used or another factor may have been to blame, but you won't be able to be sure.

Note, one big drawback to a bioassay is time. You need to plan an additional 30 or so days for the experiment to run its course before you can bring in compost from the source. It is best, in my view, just to source from operations that will fully guarantee, in writing, that their products are herbicide free. Some operations won't do so. If they won't, I wouldn't work with them.

9

Plants Are a Plant's Best Enemy: Living Mulches and Cover Crops

Living mulches are just that—mulches that are alive! These are a subset of cover crops and cover cropping, with one key difference— they complement and coexist with a main crop. Cover crops are used in **rotation with** harvestable crops, whereas living mulches are used in **companionship with** them. Cover crops are used **sequentially** in growing spaces—think cabbage then clover then cucumbers—while living mulches are used **simultaneously** with other plantings—think cucumbers with clover.

There is possibly no more beneficial step a grower can take to improve their soil than to cover crop it. Yes, cover crops even beat out mulches for improving your soil, and if done well, can come close to or equal mulches in terms of weed suppression. The benefits of cover crops are almost too many to list. First, they can be used with organic mulches, increasing soil shading and water retention, while significantly accelerating soil building. Imagine getting multiple percentage points gains in soil organic matter in a single year—that is what cover crops plus organic mulches can unleash. Studies show that a single, well established cover crop is equivalent to dropping ten tons of animal manure on an acre of land.

More than any other action a soil steward takes, integrating living mulches and cover crops with organic mulches is by far the best way

to improve the health of your soil in a short amount of time! You get the best of both worlds: all natural, beneficial tillage via plant roots below the mulch, decomposition of organic matter, strong soil food web activity, increased soil water retention and penetration, lower soil temperatures, and so much else, all at the same time.

Second, living mulches help conserve and cycle water and nutrients, and strengthen the entire soil food and nutrient web. Unlike surface mulches, living mulches work above and below the soil. During their growth phase, they primarily work below the soil, creating storage and space for nutrients, water, air, and habitat for the soil food web. Then, at the end of their life cycle, they work above the soil as a "green manure," a slow release, fertility rich surface topping. Such a green manure can be gently tilled into the soil by pigs or chickens, providing a free, high quality forage crop for the cleanup crew, or by people.

Next, cover crops are key to managing your soil's fertility. For those that use various fertilizers and amendments, cover crops reduce nutrient loss and runoff. Studies show that nitrogen loss, organic matter loss, and nutrient loss are significantly reduced by cover crops. Also, cover crops play an important role in keeping soil balanced. Over time, most growers tend to run a nitrogen deficit but nutrient excess, especially growers who use lots of compost such as animal manure based options. The excess nutrients, especially phosphorus and potassium, tend to build up the soil, harming plants and hurting yields. Cover crops can help cycle these excess nutrients out while providing nitrogen with no additional nutrients attached.

Also, cover crops are key to building a strong soil food web. Every root in the soil is a home for additional soil food web inhabitants and space for additional air, water, and nutrients. Each creature and microbe and root contains water, oxygen, nutrients, and more that cannot be easily lost to heavy rain or other natural forces. Living mulches help create space and storage for nutrients, water, and air in the subsoil. Certain living mulches also help fix and provide nitrogen to other plants, both current and future, and help attract or populate the soil with beneficial bacteria and microbes that persist long after the mulches depart. At the end of the growing season, all those roots break down, providing important food stuffs for soil dwellers, leaving behind wide open spaces for next season's plant roots, releasing nutrients, and building organic matter.

Even better, living mulches can coexist with other plantings when properly managed and timed. They have also, when properly selected, been found to attract and increase the number of predators that are vital to protecting plantings from pests, while also making it more difficult for pests to find their favorite plants to snack on.

Plant based approaches to weed control

- **Cover crops:** any planting used to "cover" the ground that is not usually a cash crop. Helps to prevent erosion, improve soil health, and provide a number of additional benefits to the soil and ecosystem.
- **Living mulches:** cover crop plants chosen specifically for their ability to play nice with cash crops in close plantings or in adjacent spaces without harming or hindering the main crop.
- **Companion planting:** Planting beneficial plants close to one another to improve yields, protect against diseases and pests, or provide other benefits. Plants may be edibles, herbs, flowers, or other types.
- **Intercropping:** the carefully timed and selected planting of multiple crops into a single space to increase yields while providing little space for weeds to get established.

Friend or Foe: Living Mulches and Competition

The key to using living mulches successfully is managing competitive pressures and timing of crops. In very poor soil, living mulches may not be prudent or possible alongside plantings, as the soil may not be nourishing and strong enough to support both, especially later in the season. For average or slightly below average soils, living mulches may need removed or otherwise dealt with before reaching high summer, when for long season plants such as peppers, squashes and tomatoes, the mulches can become a liability, competing for moisture and nutrients during the most stressful parts of the growing season. This decision depends heavily on both the grower's and the growing season's particular conditions.

Living mulches don't always come up in the most desirable of spots. If noticed and identified early enough, clovers and some other plants can easily be moved from an unwanted to a wanted location instead of merely weeding the young plants away. If no good place exists for transplant, they can at the least be fed to your animals or chopped and dropped as organic mulch. The latter option/approach has shown a great deal of promise on our farm, where a living mulch/cover crop is through hand tool or mechanical means or solarization reduced quickly to an organic mulch. The roots left below ground break down rapidly feeding the soil below, while the the rest of the plant feeds the soil from above.

Another key with living mulches is properly timing succession. For instance, early season crops like cabbage, broccoli, some onions, lettuces, and other greens, if put out early enough, can coexist with a living mulch. The living mulch can be started two to four weeks later than the main crop, and allowed to grow up among the planting. If done correctly, the living mulch will just start to shade and otherwise compete with the main crop at about the time the crop requires harvesting or some relief from warmer temperatures and strong sun. You can easily harvest the main crop while the living mulch remains, taking over the growing space until you are ready to turn it into a green manure a few weeks before the next planting needs the space.

Such a succession is wonderful to behold and glorious for soil building and overall productivity. It is like watching a wonderful, intricate, old world style village dance, where the various players dodge in and out and around and through each other with superb style and skill. Cool season crops give way to clovers that then get chopped and dropped to make space for peppers, which then give way to oats and other fall cover crops as frost approaches.

What Mulch to Munch?

Living mulches and cover crops have one main challenge—choice! There are SO many to choose from. Don't let that stop you from starting. At the end of the day, as they say, "just do it." The worst that can happen is you need to kill off an unwanted cover crop or living mulch to make space.

When choosing which mulches/cover crops to use, it is best to consult a few resources specific to your region and needs. Some plants will provide much needed nitrogen. Others are excellent at breaking up compaction. Some are only for warm season, others are perennials that you will need to either kill off at the right time or use stronger tools to remove once established. Some go to seed easily, others don't or won't.

Personally, our favorite living mulches are clovers. Clovers come in a host of varieties, from the short and bunchy whites to the tall and stately red. Generally, we have not had to seed much clover to get these to take up residence as a living mulch throughout our growing spaces. Instead, through careful weeding and care, and allowing paths and other places to go to seed each season, they have taken care of establishing themselves and now grow vigorously with no added labor or expense on our part.

Annuals, Perennials, and Self-seeding

Another factor to consider with cover crops is are they annual or perennial. Annuals will die back on their own when weather conditions—generally heavy frost or freezing temperatures—hit. Perennials will die back only to regrow come spring. This makes some types of perennials excellent choices for paths, but less ideal for certain types of soils and growing spaces. Some perennials, after a thorough, repeated mowing, will fall to occultation or solarization.

Next, should you allow cover crops or living mulches to go to seed? Well, it depends. For us, clovers are generally allowed to seed freely in paths, as they are easy to remove from unwanted places, and the savings on seed and time spent on establishing well populated paths, along with the nitrogen they provide to our plants, more than offsets the small amount of weeding they tend to add to nearby beds. Clovers are easily removed via solarization and occultation and don't germinate well once mulched, so for us they have not been a problem or issue. Oats, buckwheat, and most other plants we seek to knock back before they can seed, unless it is a bed that we plan to leave in cover crop all season. Then, we allow buckwheat to self-seed and succession plant itself until fall frost takes out the plants.

Cover Crop Quick Guide

1. Choose an appropriate cover crop or cover crop mix for the time of year, location, and your particular goals. For fall cover crops, make sure that you sow them at least 2–4 weeks before frost.

2. Wait for decent weather conditions. We generally like to seed a day or so before moderate rain and appropriate temperatures are on the forecast.

3. Prepare the area then broadcast the seed at recommended planting density.

4. Rake the seed lightly into the soil to protect it from birds and ensure good soil contact. If necessary, a thin straw mulch can help reduce bird predation.

5. Kill it off or knock back at the right time—generally this is at the flowering or seed head formation stage for most crops. For smaller growers, if all you have is a lawn mower or weed whacker, you may want to keep them even smaller to ensure you can knock

them back without needing to bring in special equipment. A few homesteaders I know manage them with a hand scythe!

6. If you don't incorporate the plant material into the soil, you can within a few days plant or transplant into most previously cover cropped spaces, using the cover crop biomass as mulch. If you work the material into the soil, plan to wait a few weeks to allow the material to break down before making use of the beds.

Rye, Oats, Clovers Top Field Trials

While there are an endless array of options for cover crops, rye and oats consistently—across regions, soil types and climates—top the list for low cost and high performance. Both are excellent for improving soil organic matter, as they are top crops for overall biomass production.

Clovers as well time and time again are hard to beat for their contribution to soil building and weed suppression. Since they add nitrogen and are a favorite pollinator and predator bug attractor, they are top of the list as well. So if you are asking, "What should I try first," you probably won't go wrong with these three options.

Using Living Mulches and Cover Crops to Deal with Pests and Diseases

Living mulches not only play an important role in weed suppression by gobbling up resources (light, water, nutrients), they can also help with both pests and diseases. On the pest side, living mulches confuse pests and help attract predators. A garden of endless edible vegetables, especially long beds of single species, is an invitation to pest invasion. Living mulches, along with proper diversified planting, breaks up these long runs that are so attractive to pests and allow them to spread quickly. On the predator side, living mulches, especially flowering varieties such as clovers or buckwheat help attract and provide habitat for predators that help control pests. Numerous studies now show that even small amounts of growing space—10% or so of the square footage—put into such beneficial plants can increase yields and reduce the need for pesticides, even organic ones, substantially.

In the soil, living mulches and cover crops can address some pest and disease issues. Certain plants, such as certain species of marigolds, sun hemp (*Crotalaria juncea* L), and a number of others reduce nematode populations (this generally involves working in the plant debris at the end of the season into the soil). Thus, such considerations may help inform what cover crop mix will give you the most benefit for the buck.

Some believe that certain plants, like mustards, help cleanse the soil of certain pathogens, but the studies don't seem to support this assertion. Instead, their benefits to disease control probably come from the role they play in improving the soil food web by breaking up compaction, adding organic matter, and other factors to help reduce pest and disease pressure.

Catch Crops

Another use for cover crops worth mentioning is catch crops. There are two ways to use catch crops—one is before main plantings to deal with pests, the other is after to minimize loss of soil and nutrients. We will look briefly at both.

While certain pests are attracted to many different types of plants, they generally have a few "favorites." A catch cover crop involves planting a pest's favorite to provide protection to other, susceptible plantings. Generally, the catch crop is planted a bit earlier (7–10 days) than the cash crop, so that the pests find it first. This then presents an opportunity to knock back the pests either by flaming the catch crop, applying an organic pesticide just to the catch crop, or harvesting the crop and disposing of it in a way that kills the pests.

The second application of a catch crop involves planting a cover crop very soon after harvest. So, after corn harvest, rye or oats can be planted to capture residual nitrogen and other free or excess nutrients still hanging around in the soil. This protects groundwater, while also stabilizing the soil to protect against incoming fall rains that will cause erosion. Or after sweet potato harvest, a mixed cover crop of oats and cool season clover can do similarly. Such catch crops allow you to make productive use of a space that doesn't have enough season left for a cash crop or that you don't need to otherwise use. Remember, nothing is more expensive than naked soil!

Nutrient Cycling and Recovery

A final benefit of cover crops worth mentioning and role they can play is nutrient cycling and recovery. Over the season, nutrients build up in the tissues of a cover crop. Then, as they are slowly broken down, these nutrients are released and made available. This helps keep nutrients where cash crops can best access them—in the top 2–6 inches of the soil—while also protecting them from washing out of the soil during heavy rains. Think of cover crops as a way to create your own slow release fertilizer right in your garden!

Also, if you are dealing with soil that is out of balance, cover crops can help remove excess nutrients or allow you to add or increase particular nutrients that your soil needs, such as using buckwheat or sweet clover to increase levels of phosphorous without increasing another nutrient like potassium. **With proper planning, you can roll soil amending and improvement, erosion reduction, and weed suppression all into a single task—a cover crop.**

Also, depending on your soil, over time nutrients tend to move deeper into the soil layers. Most perennial plants are relatively shallow rooted, so over time vast amounts of nutrients become unavailable to them. Incorporating deep rooted cover crops into your cover cropping rotation helps recover these otherwise unavailable nutrients.

Cover Crops and Solarization

For most cover crops and living mulches, solarization is an ineffective method of removal. If you can imagine, dropping a thick layer of insulative mulch works against creating intense heat to kill off plants. Clovers and similar spreading, shallow rooted, and relatively low biomass plants are the exception. For well established clovers, solarization may not kill them, but knock them back long enough to allow you to transplant other crops into a bed with them. During the first 7–10 days while the transplants are getting established, the clover will just begin to rebound. By the time the transplants are on their way up, the clover will just start its regrowth, and you should end up with a nice mixed bed that has the best of both worlds—a cash and cover crop occupying the same space in a synergistic manner.

We especially like this approach for tall and trellised plantings, such as cucumbers, tomatoes, peppers, luffa, and many others. The clover becomes a nice, thick, living mulch underneath the plantings.

10

Man-Made Mulches: Metal, Plastic, and Repurposed

Persistent mulches are the opposite of natural mulches—they resist decomposition and don't happen apart from modern production methods. Many are not carbon based. The ones that are contain a host of additional chemicals to turn them into polymers and other structures that resist decay instead of embracing it. Persistent mulches are controversial and for good reason. A good soil steward seeks to work with nature. Inorganic mulches tend to work against it. Yet, many regenerative and sustainable farmers use them, sometimes extensively. They do have some hard to pass by benefits, such as exceptional season extension through early season soil warming, great weed suppression, and significant water savings by reducing evaporation.

In this chapter, we will explore the most common persistent mulches. We will touch on the benefits and drawbacks of each, along with warnings where appropriate. Only you can decide which, if any, you will use in your operation. Hopefully this section will give you the tools to make better decisions about which to use, when, and why.

Metal Mulch

Yes, that's right, metal mulch. Talk about persistent! Used metal plays an important part in our growing. It allows us to suppress weeds and grass along long runs and wide spaces quickly, easily, and with minimal cost, effort, and environmental impact. Used sheet metal, from roofs or siding, is often available for free or very low cost, especially in rural areas where older buildings with metal roofs are often in need of demolition, and thus the metal is in need of removal. After storms, especially hail and other such weather events, large amounts become available in the areas affected as roofs are repaired and replaced. If scrap metal prices are low, many businesses would rather drop to someone who wants it close by than have to haul it long distances to a recycling center at a loss.

Metal mulch requires two important caveats. First, it has to be weighed down or secured properly. Strong winds meeting unsecured metal mulch means great danger for growers. A flying piece of thin metal is nothing to be trifled with. It can decapitate your crops, cut into your structures, and even injure or kill you and other creatures. Think of unsecured metal as a flying guillotine waiting for the right opportunity to get some momentum.

So, please take seriously the need to secure metal mulch. You don't want to become known as the guillotine gardener. Second, the edges are sharp, so it does create the need for greater care in your growing spaces and caution, especially if you like to go barefoot in the garden. Ramming a toe into a sharp piece of metal will be an experience you won't soon forget. Stitches are a definite possibility if you connect with a sheet at pace. So, when you lay sheets and weigh them down, it is important to try and make sure the edges are smooth and tight against the ground. Did I mention we keep extensive medical kits on our farm? Thankfully, we have never needed them because of the metal mulch.

We mainly use metal mulch near the edges of growing spaces, such as under fences, Sometimes we use it to buy us some time before we get a chance to put down organic mulches like straw or wood chips. In just a few minutes we can metal mulch down multiple hundreds of square feet of space that otherwise could create real problems later.

Metal Mulch, Soil, and Pests

Metal mulch has an interesting effect on soil building. On the one hand, it won't be adding significant amounts of organic matter or other things to the soil, since it isn't breaking down. If placed on top of taller grass, it will create some breakdown and soil improvement as the existing plant life is smothered and rots down. Metal mulch may provide some excellent habitat for beneficials, especially snakes, frogs, toads, and similar creatures, if some moisture is able to collect underneath. At the same time, it also provides habitat for many unwanted critters in the rodent family. Depending on the color, metal mulch can either warm or cool the soil, and increase for sun loving plants the amount of solar gain they receive, especially useful in spring for getting plants moving along.

In our experience, metal mulch is a mixed bag for larger pest issues, since while mice and voles like living under it, snakes like it even more, as do toads, frogs, and other friendly creatures. Depending on your situation, moving the metal mulch at appropriate times to disturb problematic critters and open them up to predation may be necessary. Cats and other rodent control measures make a big difference if using metal mulch to keep mice and similar populations in check. Come winter, metal mulch should be removed to not provide protected habitat for pests.

Precious Metal for Pennies

Metal mulch may be able to be acquired for little to no cost. Sometimes, older buildings are available to be disassembled for free to those willing to do the labor. Online websites such as Freecycle and Craigslist sometimes have such items available and also serve as a place where the aspiring farmer or gardener can at least ask around to see if any is available along with some other valuable and often free farm and homestead infrastructure. Depending on one's locale and economic factors, such as the value of scrap metal, a grower may or may not be able to acquire any sizable amount of metal.

I have a neighbor who is a roofer and I can for free or very low cost (especially since scrap metal is scraping the bottom of the barrel price-wise currently) get an entire load for metal mulch purposes and other farm projects.

Another way to get extra metal is finding a place that sells roofing metal and checking to see if they sell the cover sheets or otherwise damaged seconds at a discount. Cover sheets are sheets that are tossed on stacks of roofing metal to protect the sheets during transit. These are often discounted by half or more over their normal price. Same with damaged sheets or seconds—they will often be available at around half price.

Plastic Mulch (Plasticulture)

Plastic mulches have become very popular among many organic and conventional growers, especially larger operations, since they are National Organic Program (NOP) approved. They also conserve water, warm up the subsoil rapidly in early spring (thus allowing for much earlier planting than is otherwise possible), and reduce labor immensely in terms of weeding. They have also been found to increase crop yields and crop quality (Miles et al. 2012; Corbin et al., 2009). The water conservation of such a mulch should not be lightly dismissed, especially given some of their most prevalent places of use are also some of our nation's most drought prone and stricken.

For some pests, plastic mulch (and geotextiles) does provide the perfect habitat. A number of growers report that squash bugs especially like the safety plastic mulches provide, but this pest is not alone in seeking sanctuary safely tucked inside the plastic. Also, weeds will gladly grow out from under the edges of the plastic. It is also possible, especially for certain strong, aggressive weeds, or if the plastic is applied too late, for weeds to grow through it, creating punctures that if not quickly dealt with can easily undo any benefits. A breach in the plastic dam can quickly turn into a flood of weedy foes.

Plastic mulch requires the placement of drip tape or similar irrigation underneath. This increases both the expense and the labor involved in setting such beds up. Remember, the labor is two-fold—at the end of the season, all this infrastructure may need removed after you have pulled the plastic. Having had some experience helping farmers remove the plastic and irrigation at the end of the season, it can be a frustrating task depending on your soil type and quite time consuming. Laying the plastic, especially for longer runs or at larger scale, requires specialized equipment as well. Smaller operations will need to either borrow or rent for it to make financial sense.

Also, to some in the organic and permaculture movement, plastic mulches arouse significant opposition and frustration. By nature, "plasticulture" and organic agriculture sit at opposite ends of the spectrum. Polyethylene plastic mulches also have significant environmental drawbacks.

Recycling of agricultural plastics does not occur in most regions, and is usually limited by the contamination of the plastic after field use, the lack of specialized baling equipment, and the long distance to recycling facilities. (Garthe and Kowal, 1993)

The disposal of polyethylene mulches raises many concerns. In 2004, 143,000 tons of plastic mulch were disposed of in the U.S., either in the landfill or burned on site (Shogren and Hochmuth, 2004). This amount of plastic mulch, measuring four feet wide and 1 mil thick, would wrap around the earth over 100 times. On-site burning of polyethylene mulch can also have undesirable environmental impacts, such as the release of the airborne pollutant dioxane; and the practice is illegal in the U.S.

Plastic mulch also has the obvious drawback of not contributing to the soil food web and soil building. While it suppresses weeds, it also stops beneficial garden plants from taking root at the same time.

Plastic mulch does not support the use of living and organic mulches alongside crops.

Also, while plastic mulches allow rapid soil heating in late winter and early spring, they continue to keep the heat on high all summer, which is great for some plants but not for others. Thus, some growers then have the additional cost and labor to lay white plastic on top of the black plastic, using even more plastic. Or they have to apply an organic mulch, usually straw, over the plastic mulch to provide some relief to the plant's roots and soil.

Organic and sustainable growers I have spoken with at length about this issue are deeply divided. Many local organic farmers lack enough affordable labor or access to sufficient natural mulches to make replacing black plastic mulch possible or feasible. Some also have significant concerns about the delay in planting that will take place without the soil warming benefits of the plastic. Without the black plastic mulch, they believe they would be unable to make a decent living. These are real concerns that need careful consideration and for those who are not farming for a living, cannot be lightly dismissed.

At the same time, they dislike the mulches, and hope truly organic, biodegradable options soon come to market. While biodegradable options are allowed under European and Canadian certified organic standards, they are not in the United States currently.

Some larger scale growers have transitioned away from plastic mulches growing their own mulches in place, even acquiring specialized equipment that allows them to plant directly into mulch as deep as twelve inches or more. These innovations in cover cropping, roller/crimping then direct planting are promising, but not perfected, and are not inexpensive. For smaller scale growers and operations, such specialized equipment doesn't currently make economic sense.

For small scale gardeners and homesteaders (a few thousand square feet of growing space), there is generally little benefit or need to utilize plastic mulches, save possibly for very particular crops if you find yourself in a cooler climate that otherwise wouldn't allow them (peppers, tomatoes and the like). For those with multi-acre operations, the issues at play quickly become complex and require careful planning and decision making to ensure each grower is doing the best possible with what is available to them. If a small scale grower does decide to go with an inorganic mulch, geotextile is superior to plastic in my opinion. But organic and living mulches are always best, if possible.

Are biodegradable plastic mulches better?

Some growers will use the biodegradable plastic mulches. Some will use a pre-emergent herbicide coupled with the mulch to improve its effectiveness. While biodegradable plastic mulches have many of the issues of regular plastic mulch, they also have additional problems—early failure and insufficient decomposition. First, many growers report that they often start to decompose weeks or month before the growing season ends. This can create all sorts of headaches in the fall as weeds start to germinate and still have enough time to seed before winter. Hence why some growers use pre-emergent weed control chemicals with these mulches. Thus, you now have the expense and labor of both the plastic and the weed control chemicals.

Second, they need to be tilled in at the end of the season or otherwise composted. Many growers report that this process doesn't always go according to plan, with some pieces of the mulch sticking around for many, many months before it finally breaks down. As one grower put it, "It looks ugly in the field." Thus, your nice growing areas will look littered with plastic trash at the end of each season, not something most growers want!

Geotextiles: Landscape Fabric, Ground Cloth, and Other Options

Many growers highly recommend landscape fabric or other geotextiles as a mulch. Overall, this is very similar to the plastic mulch many growers use, but generally more durable/longer lasting. Whereas plastic mulch generally gives at best a single season, geotextile mulches can last three to five years or more. Many growers report ten years of use. This represents significant cost and environmental savings over plasticulture.

Geotextiles come in various sizes, and you generally want to use a size that is slightly larger than your bed size (so, for 30 inch beds, 36 inch fabric width). They also come in many names—woven ground cover, heavy duty ground cover, landscape fabric, and more.

While plastic mulch is easy to cut holes into for planting, geotextiles require a different tactic. Burning is the most efficient method to put holes in the fabric. An added bonus is you can burn through multiple sheets at a time if the planting pattern is the same for each sheet. The process is simple. Using chalk, mark out the planting pattern on the top sheet of landscape mulch. Once the pattern is marked, use a modified propane torch or a Tiger torch to burn the holes. Some people will even make a metal jig to speed up the process and protect the material from mistakes. If a torch is not available, a few growers will heat an appropriate sized round piece of metal (2.5 to 3 inch holes are perfect for most transplants).

Curtis Stone has an excellent YouTube video showing exactly how to efficiently and accurately accomplish this technique. Note, cutting is not recommended as it can result in the fabric unraveling. Burning melts the individual strands together, ensuring that the integrity of the textile is maintained.

Issues and additional warnings

Some growers report issues with temperature gain in very warm, sunny climates. Landscape fabric is also available in white, sometimes referred to as "reflective ground cover" for this reason. Or in areas where temperatures are harder to predict from year to year, growers will cover the fabric with straw or mulch to reduce heat gain during the height of summer, or roll out white fabric on top of the black. A few places even sell white/black ground cover—one side is white, one black.

Also note, it is very important to get the fabric tight and secure against the ground. Flapping fabric can damage or kill transplants and can damage established plants, not to mention damage the fabric itself. Also note, for those that are certified organic, the fabric must be removed at the end of the season and stored. This isn't a bad idea, since it will significantly increase the fabric's life.

Realize, there is a wide range of materials that fall under the name geotextiles and landscape fabric—woven ground cover, heavy duty ground cover, weed barrier fabric, and more—so make sure you get the right stuff. If you are not sure, ask the seller and also ask how many years the material is rated for and for what applications it is designed.

Pests and diseases

Like with plasticulture, certain pests may find the protected space underneath geotextiles makes an inviting home. This can also make dealing with them without resorting to chemicals, including organic ones, difficult. Also, especially for lettuces, some diseases may build up in the fabric, waiting to infect a subsequent crop. Occasional sanitation of the fabric is recommended and required, usually once every 2–3 crops or **any time** a previous crop was beset by a disease problem.

To sanitize the geotextile, a rubbermaid watering tote works very well. You can either use regular bleach or an organic sanitizer such as Benefact or SaniDate.

Trellising, Plasticulture, and Geotextiles

A final issue to note. With both geotextiles and plasticulture, some approaches to trellising won't work or may create the need for adjustments or workarounds to get them to work properly. With geotextiles, you will need to burn the holes not just for plants, but also for any trellising or supports the plants will need. Some types of support, like cages, may not work well or may damage the plastic or textile. In high tunnels and greenhouses, where support for plants is often done from the top down, this is generally not an issue; but in the field, proper trellising with these approaches to weed control is very important. Plasticulture is generally easier to work with, as you can just drive support poles, t-posts, or similar trellising supports right through after making a small slit. If there aren't too many posts per linear foot, you can also do the same with geotextiles as well instead of burning additional holes.

Miscellaneous Mulches

There are a few more persistent mulches worth mentioning before we finish our long foray into mulches. The main thing all the remaining mulches we will discuss have in common is that they tend to be incredibly persistent and highly unnatural, cast offs from modern consumerism industry and low cost, high profit, slick marketed stuff that needs some sort of disposal. Disposing of it as yet another opportunity to snag sales from unsuspecting consumers is certainly not stooping below what many are willing to do in the modern economy.

They share the same problem as the above mulches: they don't feed the soil food web and build soil over time. But they have additional issues—many contain chemicals that actually harm the soil food web and hamper soil building, while also leaving heavy metals and other toxins and contaminants in our growing spaces.

Ground up rubber mulch (tire crumbs, crumb rubber)

It is non-allergenic, non-toxic and harmless to plants, pets, and children.

—Brad A. Pittam, general manager of LTR Products, a
division of Liberty Tire Recycling

Tire crumbs, also known as crumb rubber, is made by removing the metal belts inside of tires and grinding the leftover rubber. I have received enough questions about it (especially because of the slick lies, I mean advertising, like you see in the above quote) that it requires mentioning.

Its most common applications are on playgrounds and landscaping areas around homes. In both, studies have shown a genuine cause for concern. Tire crumbs release a host of various chemicals used in tire production—volatile organic chemicals, polyaromatic hydrocarbons, 2-mercaptobenzothiazole, and the like. Rubber mulch has also been shown to leach chemicals and various metals into the soil below the mulch—cadmium, chromium, aluminum, copper, iron, manganese, molybdenum, selenium, sulfur, and zinc. A number of research facilities have found especially high zinc levels, since tires contain up to 2% zinc by weight. The USDA agricultural research service has after twenty years of research, based primarily on the zinc issue alone, stated that rubber mulch should **never** be used in landscaping or gardens. Strange that it is allowed for our children's play areas and schools.

Rubber mulches are also, if ignited, very difficult to extinguish while not being nearly as effective as natural mulches at preventing erosion or suppressing weeds.

One study found ten metals and up to twenty five chemicals leached out from the rubber mulch. Thus, while adaptive reuse and recycling are important, it appears recycled tire crumbs are not a good example. Who benefits from this mulch? Follow the money. The companies who make it, selling tire chips and crumbs at over forty times what they can get for them in more appropriate, industrial applications.

For growers, as well as the general warning against their use, I bring up tire crumbs because they may be a **common additive in some commercial compost.** Yes, some companies and compost producers add ground up waste tires to their compost systems as a cheap bulking agent, similar to how large food companies add what were once considered waste products to processed foods because of their low cost and ability to bulk up the item cheaply (and thus bulk up their profits at the same time). Even better, it, like so many dangerous and noxious things added to food and consumer products, can be hidden under some lovely fuzzy labeling lingo. Look for things like "bulking agents" or some other imprecise and obscuring term.

Plywood and chipboard

Because used plywood boards abound, some growers use them for mulching paths or around beds. The problem with such an application is the unknown amount of preservative chemicals originally applied and then still retained in the plywood. Plywood can contain anywhere from .2 to .41 or more pounds of chemical preservatives per cubic foot. Plywood rated for greater exposure to the elements will contain more chemicals. Once the plywood is placed in the moist, warm environment outdoors and in direct contact with the soil, these chemicals begin to leach out and breakdown into the soil.

One of the main chemicals contained in plywood is copper azole. It is both a fungicide and insecticide. Given the importance of fungi and insects to the soil food web, it is best to avoid laying down plywood mulches that may release chemicals into the soil and air and harm the creatures so crucial to long term soil health. It is just one, though, of many chemicals with both known and unknown risks to both human, plant, animal, and microbial wellbeing. This is another mulch I would suggest to avoid making use of in your operation.

Used carpet

Some growers have access to large amounts of used carpet and use it to mulch and even create small water features on their properties and farms. Personally, I cannot recommend using carpet in food growing spaces. Carpets are made with glues, dyes, flame retardants, and a host of other chemicals. While these do breakdown and dissipate over time, until a thorough study is done on their effects on and accumulation in the soil, I would, here again, urge growers to take caution and steer clear.

Also, similar to a few other only semi-effective mulches, some weeds and grasses will grow right through carpet. Once they do, removing either the weeds or the carpet becomes a Herculean feat of endless frustration. While there may be some creative reuse ideas for old carpet, mulch and weed suppression isn't one of them.

Landscaping cloth/landscape fabric

Some growers have tried landscaping cloth to suppress weeds, but discovered quickly that many weeds will grow right through it. Once weed riddled, its removal makes facial hair tweezer plucking seem peachy in comparison.

The stuff is, like so many things for sale, a boon for oil companies and international conglomerates, but a doom to the soil food web and growers. The drawbacks are numerous. It doesn't do a very good job of suppressing weeds. It is recommended to top dress with an organic mulch, which after a few years, breaks down into a perfect place for weeds to germinate on top of said landscape fabric, and thus makes it even more difficult to remove while stopping this wonderful organic material from reaching the soil below where it is needed and can interact with the soil food web and soil building cycle. When, not if, you get weeds, they will penetrate the cloth from above this time, entangling their roots into its tiny woven strands, making removing a struggling child high on Pixy Stix or Skittles from a carseat seem a feat of immense ease by comparison. In a nutshell, it doesn't work, and it makes any other work far worse.

Installing landscape fabric makes landscapers lots of money, but honest ones warn clients against it. High quality ones won't offer it at all. Sometimes it is recommended for soil stabilization, but studies have shown organic mulches are better, especially since they increase plant transplant success and speed of growth, which establishes the true erosion protector and preventer: plants, roots, and the soil food web.

Part Three

Taking the Battle to the Weeds and Seeds

To win against weeds, it isn't enough to try and crowd them out or eat those that you can get your hands on and sink your teeth into. You need to take the battle to them. You need to find ways to reduce their population and make them waste their resources so that they don't have energy to reproduce. This is where forced germination, occultation, and solarization come in. They are three of the most cost and time effective ways to get weeds under control and reduce your soil seed bank. They also have other benefits to boot—helping reduce pests and diseases or warming the soil in the early season so you can get things into the ground sooner than otherwise.

11

Organize Your Army!

Growers have a wide range of tools at their disposal to stop weeds from taking over their territory. I like to think of them as my own private, anti-weed army. In general, I just need to deploy them properly and they will do most of the work for me. This involves a number of tools and tactics—tight plant spacing, companion planting, creating understories, and more.

Harnessing a Plant Army to Suppress Resistance

Empty space is an invitation to a weed invasion. So, the first goal for growers is to ensure that your growing spaces provide no foothold for weeds to get going in. This involves a number of techniques, including dense plantings, intercropping, companion planting, and undersowing. Each technique has different crop combinations and circumstances where it works best, so we will include examples of how we and others use each.

Let's look at each technique and how to apply it.

Tight Patterns and Spacing

The spacing used for planting can make a big difference in how much weeding it will need. Combined with an appropriate mulch, proper spacing can eliminate 90% or more of the work **for some crops**. Take broccoli—Cornell university found that broccoli planted as tightly as

8x10 inches per plant suffered no yield loss, but also faced almost no weed pressure **once established**. Compare that spacing to the standard recommendation of 15–18 inches apart per plant and 18–24 inches between rows! You are looking at 80 square inches per plant compared to 240 square inches per plant—Cornell gave plants 1/3 as much space with no loss to the yield and fantastic weed work reduction!

The best plants to use with this approach are broccoli, cabbage, lettuces, kales and a number of other greens. Each of these plants helps shade and crowd out weeds below once established **if** you follow a tight planting pattern. Also, many varieties of lettuces and other greens are now available that grow more upright, allowing tight row spacing to not only increase yields per square foot, but crowd out weeds as well.

Let's look at one crop in particular—cabbage. Instead of two parallel rows in a single bed, we plant three offset rows, creating an X pattern.

Imagine two rows of cabbage, planted 18 inches apart for the rows.

Traditional planting: parallel rows race car style. X = plants, O = empty space

```
X   X   X   X   X
  0   0   0   0
X   X   X   X   X
```

Notice the problem? Such parallel planting means the plants crowd each other along the row while creating a big hole (denoted by the O) in the space between. You reduce your yields per square foot while increasing your weeds, because the plants will run into each other at the tips, but leave that center space mostly empty.

But if we plant like this instead:

```
X   X   X   X   X
  X   X   X   X
X   X   X   X   X
```

Notice that you fill that hole between rows with plants. Since many plants grow in a relatively circular shape, the amount of uncovered space is minimized. With some plants, if you get the spacing just right, there is no uncovered soil at all!

The only difference between the two approaches? The spacing. We will do these rows 12 inches apart instead of 18. The total is still 36 inches for the bed, but by offsetting the plants we will fit **more** plants per square foot in the bed while creating **less** open space for weeds. It is a win-win.

You can do offset planting with two, three, four, even five rows, depending on the size of your beds and the plant in question. The one danger with doing more than three or four is plant checks, pest control, and problems harvesting. Some plants, like cabbage, especially if you are using row cover, do well in wider beds with many rows. But for most, stick with at most 3–5 rows per bed.

It takes some experimentation to get the spacing right. Note that it depends on the varieties you like to grow, since different cabbages, for instance, require different spacing. Once you sort it out, the increased yields and decreased weeds make it more than worth it. So perhaps when first starting out, plant a few beds with slightly different spacing to see what works best for your particular varieties.

Also, some plants are much better at suppressing weeds than others if spaced densely. For instance, by moving sweet potatoes slightly closer together and mulching heavily, we only need to remove a few weeds for a few weeks. After a month, the sweet potatoes so thoroughly shade the soil that almost nothing stands a chance at joining the party, and for the remainder of the season we do almost no additional weeding. This isn't true at all for things like cucumbers, which, when planted too densely, become difficult to care for and harvest.

Drawbacks and Dangers to Dense Planting Patterns

One drawback to tightly planting some crops, especially those that get direct seeded, is the need for seeders or other tools that help ensure the spacing is done properly. While some growers broadcast seed, this results in a great deal of additional seed cost **and** labor—as you have to go back and thin the planting, and you often end up with spaces that have poor plant spacing and density. Depending on your scale, a Jang or other seeder may make good sense. Transplants are another way to ensure good spacing and patterns. For long beds, you can use T-posts, rebar, or even heavy duty sticks at each end of the bed with a rope tied across to ensure you keep the pattern and spacing straight and square.

Two other issues are also worth mentioning. In the Cornell study, they provided both irrigation (as needed) and supplemental fertilization throughout the growing season. If your soil is very good, you may be able to plant more densely with no yield loss, but it isn't a bad idea to have some fish emulsion or other fertilizers on hand in case a dense planting looks like it is lacking sufficient nutrients. With the irrigation issue, dense plantings don't dry out as well or quickly, so drip tape or a similar approach to providing supplemental water (if needed) is recommended.

Superhuman Seeding: The Benefit of Pelleted Seed

Ever just about lose your salvation working with small size seeds? Lettuce, carrots, and other tiny crops that cause you to curse and cuss because they are so uncooperative? If you have to hand seed or use a less expensive seeder, one way to make it easier and more accurate is to purchase pelleted seed. These are seeds that are coated in an organic approved shell that makes them far easier to handle and plant accurately. While they cost more than standard seeds—they are anywhere from 2–4x more expensive—they are absolutely worth the additional cost, especially if you are purchasing more than a packet of seeds at a time. First, you save a fair amount of seeds using pelleted. Between dropped, lost, sticking to the packet flap and all the other issues with many small seed varieties, we found that we were often losing a fair amount of seed right off the bat. This is almost completely eliminated with pelleted seed.

Second, because your planting is more accurate, there should be little to no need to spend time thinning later, and the better spacing means better yields and less weeds. If you go from thinning 1/3 of what you plant to nothing, that is a significant labor and seed savings. So, we have found that even with the additional upfront cost, pelleted seeds result in large savings compared to regular when we factor in seed costs, yields, and labor together.

One note, pelleted seed has a shorter shelf life than standard seeds because of the additional moisture added during the pelleting process. Plan to use them the same growing season/year you purchase them. Refrigeration will slightly increase their storage life—by about six additional months, enough to use them at the beginning of the next season. Plan on slightly poorer germination rates, though.

Saving on seeds

Purchasing garden seed by the packet is a pricey proposition. It is astronomically cheaper to order larger amounts of seed. I suggest people find other like-minded growers to split seeds with for this reason. A single packet of lettuce costs around $5 and contains 1000 seeds. An ounce costs around $15, but contains over 30,000 seeds! That is 3x the cost for 30 times the seed!

Here you see how to afford pelleted seed, since at larger scales the cost per seed drops substantially, as does the premium over regular seed.

Napoli Carrot: $4.55/750 seeds → 21.10/10,000 seeds (5x cost for 15x the seed!)

Napoli Pelleted: $5.40/250 seeds → 32.10/10,000 seeds (6x the cost for 40x the seed!)

Note how for pelleted seed, as you purchase larger quantities, the cost difference over regular seed drops substantially! 10,000 pelleted seeds are only 50% more, compared to 250 pelleted seeds being over 300% more per seed!

Intercropping

A second way to reduce weeds and increase yields takes advantage of the differing speeds at which many plants grow. Some crops are space hogs in a garden, but take a long time to actually make use of all that room. Such crops leave a great deal of open space for weeds to take up residence in in the meantime. What is a grower to do? Intercropping is an excellent option.

Intercropping generally involves pairing a slow growing crop with a fast growing crop. Both get planted at roughly the same time. By the time the fast growing crop is ready to harvest, the slow growing crop is ready to expand into what will soon be empty space. Radishes and carrots are one common example. Radishes grow very quickly, while carrots take almost twice as long to reach harvest. By the time the carrots are ready for prime time, the radishes are ready to harvest, opening up space, water, and sun for the carrot crop.

Another example is a scaled down "three sisters," using various types of beans, especially drying bush bean varieties, underneath corn. The beans help keep the corn patch weeded, add valuable nitrogen for the next year's crop, and provide other benefits including a harvestable crop at the end of the season. Some plants, such as leeks or green onions, can have lettuce intercropped between them. The strong scent of these alliums provides some protection against pests for the lettuces. Intercropping is becoming more and more popular with those that grow grains. The number of pairings is endless, and is especially driven by location, soil type, and other factors.

Field trials of intercropping show that not only does it improve total yields and profitability per square foot or acre, but it also may improve each individual crop's yields. Also, some intercrop pairings were found to reduce both diseases and pest pressures on the partner crops. For instance, bean fly was found to be significantly deterred when the beans were intercropped with leeks.

Also note, intercropping can be used to provide shade for a main crop. So, we have intercropped flowers with some of our cooler season greens, such as spinach and kale, to provide some relief from the long, sunny summer days we have in Kentucky that sometimes come hot and early. The spinach will still receive more than enough sunlight, while the shade will reduce stress on the plants.

Some intercropping options and examples

- Radishes with carrots or lettuce
- Overwintered spinach into peas
- Lettuce with broccoli, kale, or cauliflower
- Chard with lettuce or scallions
- Dill with cabbage or broccoli
- Dry beans with corn
- Cotton with melons
- Onions or garlic into squash or other summer crops
- Kale, broccoli and similar brassicas to fall lettuce and salad mixes (if your season is shorter, farther south, many of our brassicas never make it past mid summer).

What is the Difference Between Intercropping and Companion Planting?

You might say, hey, this looks or sounds a lot like companion planting. You are right. Intercropping is similar to companion planting. Yet, there are a few differences. Most of the differences are small, involving issues of closeness, timing, and plant choice.

First, proximity. Companion planting is often done with a bit more distance than intercropping. Sometimes it is done by alternating beds of beneficial plants, or making rows of companion plants along the sides of a main crop. Intercropping involves tightly placing two crops together, often in alternating, tightly seeded rows. In companion planting you have a bed of carrots with radishes on the outside—in intercropping you have radishes planted in between your rows of carrots, with little to no change to your row spacing for the carrots!

Second, timing. With intercropping, there is often a goal to have one crop harvested and out of the way of the other crop at a particular time when the second crop will need the additional space. This is sometimes done by planting two crops with very different growth rates in alternating rows. It is also done by planting into space between an existing crop that still has some time left before it is harvested or otherwise peters out.

This is very different from companion planting, where the two or more crops tend to co-exist together for a large part of the season in a mutually beneficial relationship (though not always!), like basil with tomatoes, or oregano with cucumbers or peppers. You should view intercropping as another tool that takes a bit more care and precision to pull off properly in a growing space. But it is one with incredible benefits, especially if you are limited on space or trying to produce as much dollar value per square foot as possible.

Leave No Ground Un-greened: Companion Plants and Undersowing

One of my favorite growing mottos is simple—if you can see the ground, you didn't plant enough! By the summer solstice, my goal is to turn our entire growing space into a dense, green jungle of happy plant matter. Other than spots that were solarized, every square foot should be filled with dense foliage. There are two main ways we make this happen—companion planting and undersowing.

Companion planting

In nature, plants don't grow in uniform isolation, a row of grass here, clover there, twenty nicely arranged oaks then thirty neatly space maples. Instead, they grow in a mixed up mess of vegetative madness. While total chaos isn't my recommendation, a diverse uniformity, or a uniform diversity, or some mixture therein is what we should aim for.

Companion planting often comes with various rules. Not all plants play nice next to one another. Plants are like kids—some just shouldn't sit next to each other on the schoolbus! Also, some plants appear to have synergistic, mutually beneficial relationships when placed in close proximity to certain other plants. Others go full Hatfield and McCoy if not given sufficient space from one another.

Companion planting charts abound. Take these with a grain of salt and as a starting point for experimentation. While some companion planting pairings are based on solid research and reasoning, we and other growers have found that some are not.

Undersowing

Many plants that grow up instead of out are perfect candidates for undersowing. In this technique, we allow a trellised crop—such as tomatoes, peppers, cucumbers—a head start over a shorter understory, especially nice, dense, soil benefiting ground covers like clover. The clover benefits the cucumbers and soil—adding nitrogen, attracting pollinators, improving water penetration, and cooling the ground, among other benefits. But it doesn't interfere with or inhibit the trellised crop, which rises above its ground support to the sunny spaces above.

In a sense, undersowing and sometimes companion planting are modified approaches to cover crops, which we talked about at length in the mulch section. The goal of such crops is to improve soil; protect against erosion, rain, and sun; provide food and habitat for beneficial creatures; help deter or repel pests; and more.

Nature abhors a vacuum. If there is space, something is going to want to grow in it. The question is will you decide or will nature do it for you? As much as possible, we want to plant as tightly and densely as our soil and water resources will allow, so that there is as little free space as possible for freeloading weeds to take up residence in. Here is a good rule of thumb—our goal is to make it so only green and no ground is showing in our growing spaces.

If you have a large growing space, this is where a precision seeder, such as a Jang or similar machine can make a big difference. It is hard to make nice, tight stands with hand seeding, especially with smaller seeded crops. For us smaller growers or homesteaders who don't yet own such equipment, there is another solution—pelleted seed. Pelleted carrot, lettuce, and other seeds make even planting much easier. They also reduce our labor, since it eliminates the tedious thinning that many small seeded crops require.

12

Forced Germination

It is February 15th and we are weeding. The nighttime temperatures are often below freezing, but yet we are weeding. It is many weeks until anything can go into the ground, but we are weeding. We may not be planting this space for two or more months, yet we are weeding. How did we get the weeds to come up even though the ground is often still frozen? Forced germination.

Combine low tech materials with micro-climate trickery and you can turn late winter into weeds' and grasses' worst nightmare. Using clear, heavy duty UV stabilized plastic (greenhouse is what we use), we wait for an opportune stretch of weather—recent rains followed by a warm spell lasting three or so days with as much sun as possible. Generally, we want day time temperatures to get into the low 40s or 50s, with full to mostly sunny conditions, but even the high 30s will often work. While we prefer clear plastic, some growers will use dark tarps to encourage germination. Either will work—in our experience, the clear works better, but if all you have is black, don't hesitate to try it instead.

On the morning of the warm, sunny weather, we pull plastic over the space we hope to treat. We bury the edges to trap in the heat and warm the soil as much as possible. Then, we wait, leaving the plastic in place for 10–14 days to ensure as much germination as possible. Then, we pull the plastic. The ground should be covered in innumerable young plants—the children of last years crops along with all sorts of other progeny from the soil's seed bank.

At this point, there are three ways to deal with the young plants.

1. Let nature take care of them—**if it will get cold enough to kill the plants**, why not let nature do your dirty work for you? Note that for this to work, you want to pull the plastic or tarp during the **coldest** weather possible, preferably below freezing. You don't want to allow the plants to harden off during mild days, so keep them protected until a nice cold snap is forecasted. Plan to go through and deal with any remaining plants that the weather didn't take care of for you.

2. Let animals take care of them—chickens enjoy young greens and their nibbling and scratching will often quickly clean up an area. Timing is critical—too long a stay will turn up more seeds, too little may not take out all the ones present. Also, remember your food safety rules—once chickens have touched the space, you can't harvest anything from it for ninety or more days.

3. Let you take care of them—use a rake, cultivator, or similar tool to lightly work just the top 1/2 to 1 inch of soil to uproot the weeds. You can also use a flame weeder. Note that some companies now sell specialized rakes specifically for clearing beds of young, newly emergent weeds.

As mentioned earlier, I don't recommend tillage, as tillage not only reduces soil health and creates other problems, it also turns up buried weed seeds, undoing all the work you just did to force germinate. If you use hand tools, the goal is to go light, disturbing only the top quarter to half inch of so of the soil. For this, I like to use a nice garden rake's backside. It allows me to quickly clean a bed in just a few passes while staying super shallow on the soil.

Forced germination is an excellent technique for those in climates and situations that allow it. Since it is done during the off season, it doesn't disrupt your growing schedule or add additional work during the busy growing season. It does take preparation so that when a window of weather pops up, you can take full advantage of it.

Also, it is a technique you can do repeatedly on a space with no ill effects. Leave one side of the plastic buried when you go to remove the weeds, so that you can then quickly reset it for a second round of treatment on the same spot if needed or wanted. It is also a way to help a cover crop get going earlier than weather would normally permit—once it germinates, uncover it during milder weather to allow it to harden off, then remove the tarp and let it do its amazing cover crop magic. If your climate and schedule permits, a few cycles of light cultivation followed by forced germination is one way to reduce the seed bank substantially off-season.

While it is a good tool to take advantage of, in our experience it works best to help reduce cool, early season weeds in our location. Many varieties won't cooperate with a February, March, or early April wake up call. Also, it does little to weaken or kill off rhizome and some other hardy, noxious weed species—indeed, it can make those worse by giving them a head start going into spring. For those, and for true weed annihilation, we next turn our attention to the ultimate, all natural weed removal technique—solarization.

How to force germinate

- **Watch for an appropriate stretch of weather:** Mostly sunny to full sun and warm (above freezing) is best.
- **Prep area:** If needed, mow space thoroughly—plastic should be as close to the ground as possible. Any woody debris, sticks, or similar material that may puncture the plastic should be removed.
- **Apply tarp to area:** Make sure edges are buried or that the tarp is secured/weighted down properly.

- **Wait 10–14 days:** You can check an edge of the tarp or look under the plastic to see if things are moving along and plants are germinating.
- **Pull tarp:** Remove tarp and use one of the methods outlined above to take care of the young plants.

13

Solarization: Let the Sun do the Work for You

Plants love sunlight. It is what makes them grow, grow, grow. But put a window on top of a section of grass in the middle of summer and watch what happens. That same sun goes from blessing to bane in just a few hours. After a few days, the earth is scorched and barren, the plants reduced to nothing but dead residue. Such is the power of the sun. It is a power we can use to improve our soil while removing problematic weeds and weed seeds at the same time.

Instead of covering your garden in old, used heavy windows or panes of glass, growers can use clear, UV stabilized greenhouse plastic to solarize the soil—that is, trap incoming solar energy to raise the temperature of the soil to above 120 degrees.

Solarization is an incredibly beneficial tactic for weed control, because it also:

1. Reduces soil borne pathogens and pests and pest eggs, including nematodes.

2. Reduces both annual and perennial weeds and weed seeds, along with weakening or even killing shallow to moderately deep rooted rhizome reproducing plants and perennials.

3. Is efficient and quick to apply to large areas (2000–4000 square feet) labor-wise.

4. Is very effective against shallow rooted, fast spreading, and often very problematic weeds like Creeping Charlie and crabgrass.

If there is one tactic I wish I would have learned about sooner when it comes to weed control, this would be it. Aside from mulching, I have found no better way to deal a death blow to large amounts of weeds and weed seeds and other unwanted plants in growing spaces, with so little labor and such high rates of success. It is why for those in mid to southern locations, I consider solarization the king of weed control. No other technique comes close to its effectiveness.

How Does Solarization Work?

Every day, the sun bathes the earth in immense amounts of energy. Normally, the earth responds by producing an abundance of beautiful plants that absorb the incoming energy, turning it into biomass of all shapes and sorts. With solarization, we seek to collect and concentrate that incoming energy to raise temperatures in the soil to levels that destroy weeds and grasses, seeds of all sorts, and even rhizome reproducing root systems up to four or more inches deep. It is the end of the weeds as we know it, and about this I feel fine!

As an added bonus, solarization also removes or reduces certain pest populations and soil borne pathogens. Solarization is excellent at removing fusarium, nematodes, lightly burrowing plant pests that stay in the top 4–6 inches of the soil, along with their eggs and offspring, among many other diseases and pests. At the same time, it has a net positive impact on the soil's overall health **if done properly**, only temporarily disrupting the soil food web and doing so in a way that actually long term allows it to flourish.

Solarization during the hot summer months can increase soil temperature to levels that kill many disease causing organisms (pathogens), nematodes, and weed seeds and seedlings. It leaves no toxic residues and can be easily used on a small or large scale garden or farm. Soil solarization also speeds up the breakdown of organic material in the soil, often resulting in the added benefit of release of soluble nutrients such as nitrogen (N03⁻, NH4⁺), calcium (Ca⁺⁺), magnesium (Mg⁺⁺), potassium (K⁺), and fulvic acid, making them more available to plants.

Plants often grow faster and produce both higher and better quality yields when grown in solarized soil. This can be attributed to improved disease and weed control, the increase in soluble nutrients, and relatively greater proportions of helpful soil microorganisms.

http://ipm.ucanr.edu/PMG/PESTNOTES/pn74145.html

What Does Solarization Combat?

Solarization is very effective against a wide swath of the most common garden goons. Here is just one listing, compiled by the University of California.   (http://ipm.ucanr.edu/PMG/PESTNOTES/pni7441-tbl4.html)

Common Name	Scientific Name
barnyardgrass	Echinochloa crus-galli
bermudagrass (seed only)	Cynodon dactylon
bindweed, field (seed only)	Convolvulus arvensis
bluegrass, annual	Poa annua
Broomrape	Orobanche ramosa
chickweed, common	Stellaria media
cocklebur, common	Xanthium strumarium
crabgrass, large	Digitaria sanguinalis
fiddleneck, Douglas	Amsinckia douglasiana
goosegrass	Eleusine indica
groundsel, common	Senecio vulgaris
henbit	Lamium amplexicaule
horseweed	Conyza canadensis
johnsongrass (seed only)	Sorghum halepense
lambsquarters, common	Chenopodium album
lettuce, miner's	Clytonia perfoliata
mallow, little (cheeseweed)	Malva parvidora
mustard, black	Brassica nigra
nightshade, black	Solanum nigrum

nightshade, hairy	Solanum sarrochoides
oat, wild	Avena fatua
oxalis, buttercup	Oxalis pes-caprae
pigweed, redroot	Amaranthus retroflexus
pigweed, tumble	Amaranthus albus
purslane, common	Portulaca oleracea
purslane, horse	Trianthema portulacastrum
shepherd's-purse	Capsella bursa-pastoris
sida, prickly	Sida spinosa
sowthistle, annual	Sonchus oleraceus
velvetleaf	Abutilon theophrasti

If in doubt, assume solarization will work against most weeds and other problematic plants. The only exceptions are well established, deep rooted perennials or plants that have natural defenses against incredibly high temperatures.

Solarizing the Soil: A Blessing or a Bad Thing?

Some people often express skepticism at the idea that heating the soil to high temperatures actually benefits it. Yet, we have clear historical evidence that it indeed does. The native Americans practiced controlled burns that produced some of the biggest trees the world has ever seen along with exceptionally fertile soils and healthy ecosystems.

Solarization accomplishes similar goals, without the release of large amounts of organic matter into the air and without the dangers of fire spreading beyond the intended areas. Also, we have more than mere historical example. Modern science has shown benefits to plants, even apart from reduced pathogen and pest loads from solarized soil.

The impact of solarization on the soil food web is a complex and still debated discussion. Since many growers who use a method such as solarization to control weeds will also make use of compost and similar soil amendments, applying these post solarization is prudent, though there are also benefits to applying them *beforehand* as well. For instance, applying amendments prior to solarization can dramatically increase its effectiveness against certain pests.

Since we make both compost and vermicompost on farm, each solarized area gets a high quality, natural inoculant post treatment as we replant. If you have any concerns about the impact on the soil food web, a few simple steps will more than offset any losses that take place during the solarization process. Also, compared to the known damage and losses of other weed control methods, even if solarization does suppress certain parts of the soil food web, it does so at a fraction of the damage that other common weed control methods—especially tillage, cultivation, and chemicals—unleash.

Considerations for Successful Solarization

While solarization is a simple, low tech way to control weeds, there are a number of things to understand so that you use this technique successfully.

Preparation and installation of plastic

For the area you want to solarize, make sure your plastic is at least two feet longer on all sides. So if you want to solarize a 30x40 foot area, you will need plastic with dimensions of around 34x44 feet. If you need to do a smaller area, instead of cutting the plastic down, consider rolling up the excess. With plastic, remember this—**Once you cut it, you generally can't put it back together!** So, we try to avoid cutting our main sheet, and if we have a smaller area, keep part of the plastic rolled up on a side that won't collect water.

Also note, once you get in the 20x20 range and higher, the plastic becomes heavy. At 40x40, the plastic is very heavy and best handled by a two person crew. Avoid dragging the plastic around—it will cause abrasions and tears that greatly diminish its effectiveness.

The larger the piece of plastic, the more kite-like it will behave in the wind. So the larger the area you hope to solarize, the less windy the day you will want to do installation on, or the more people you will want on hand to help handle the tarp. All it takes is a big gust of wind for your plastic to end up in a tree like Charlie Brown's kite! The big difference? Getting your plastic down, now with complimentary holes, will be a great deal more work.

Moisture

Soil needs sufficient moisture to solarize. Overly wet, waterlogged soil and overly dry soil will not solarize properly. If it is sopping, wait for it to dry out for a few days first. If the ground is dry, add sufficient moisture before installing the plastic. The squeeze test is a good way in most soils to see if conditions are right—take a handful of soil and squeeze it in your hand. Some droplets of water should fall out. If a river runs forth, it is too wet. If the soil is dry in your hand or no droplets form, it is too dry. Soil should be moist six inches down.

Protecting the plastic!

Since solarization requires as much heat as possible to be trapped and pushed down into the soil, holes in the tarp will hinder if not outright derail or halt the process. It is very important that the tarp have no holes. It is also important that the area the tarp is applied to doesn't pose a threat to the integrity of the plastic. Even small sticks or other objects may cause punctures or tears.

Thus, before applying the tarp, it is best to mow the area thoroughly, very close to the ground. After mowing, do a walkover to remove any debris, such as sticks or any other pointy or sharp objects that pose a threat to the plastic. This will not only protect the plastic and reduce the need for repairs, but also improve the effectiveness. Each hole or rip results in an incredible amount of lost energy and heat that you want going into the soil instead of escaping back into the atmosphere.

Placing the plastic

Plastic should be placed as close and tight to the ground as possible and buried on all edges in a shallow, 4 to 6 inch deep and 4 to 6 inch wide trench. If you are starting with very poor or difficult soil, machinery may be the only means to make the trench. If this is the case, you may want to consider biosolarization outlined below or improving the soil via some other method instead of starting with solarization. Use the dirt from the trenches to secure the plastic in the trench.

Because the plastic needs to be as close to the ground as possible, reduction of surface matter through mowing and removal of any objects or features that prevent the plastic getting as close to the ground as possible is imperative. Don't skimp on proper preparation, as it can make all the difference in solarization's speed and success.

Securing the plastic

If you are doing smaller areas, especially through our strip solarization technique, and either do not want to or cannot dig a trench to secure the plastic, or are just trying to knock back easy to control plants in between crops during high summer, you can use other approaches to secure the plastic in place. I do not recommend cinder or concrete blocks, as they may puncture or otherwise damage the plastic in our experience. Instead, sandbags are a better option. These are placed every eight or so feet on both long edges of the plastic. You can secure the sandbags and the solarization tarp more tightly by tieing the sandbags together using rope. This helps keep the tarp from kicking up so much in between the sandbags during winds. If your area is especially windy, you may need to use additional bags. Err on the side of too many, as the time it takes to toss a few extra sandbags on is far less than the time it takes to chase plastic across pasture or neighboring properties.

With large areas, tossing sandbags out across the center, one to two per every hundred square feet, is recommended if you are not going to trench the edges. Remember, the larger the piece of plastic, the more kite-like it will behave in windy weather. Better a few extra sandbags than an airborne piece of expensive, heavy duty plastic! I have seen a few pictures of tarps ending up in treelines—I can only imagine the headache getting it down became for the owners, along with the innumerable holes and tears the tarp now has rendering it worthless!

For strips 6 feet in width and under, just sand bag or secure the tarp along the edges.

How Long, O Sun?

Now that the plastic is in place, you are probably wondering, "How long is this going to take?" Unfortunately, there is no simple answer. Below are the factors that can lengthen or shorten the time it takes to reduce plants, plant seeds, pathogens, and pests.

Location

The closer to the equator you are, the easier it is to solarize, the longer the windows/times of year you have to solarize, and generally the faster it will finish. The farther away from the equator you go, the shorter the windows for success. Higher elevations that result in cooler overall temperatures can slow down the process and limit the windows for effective solarization as well.

Orientation

Even if you are located farther south, the orientation of your land may limit solarization's success. Land that faces mainly south will solarize better and has a longer window for solarization than land that faces north. For us, our farm's slope means while we sit in Kentucky, our growing season is more like the middle of Indiana, a solid 150 or so miles north of our location. On the other side of the ridge, our neighbor's property acts more like the border of Kentucky and Tennessee, a hundred or so miles south, because of a gentle, perfect, southernly orientation along with an excellent windbreak of woods to the north and west.

Slope

Relatively flat land is the easiest to evenly solarize. Depending on how great the slope of your land, you may need to spread your solarization tarp fully, realizing that only the upper half will solarize properly. The bottom half may suppress and stunt weeds and grass, but will need additional treatment.

Our land fits this situation. So generally, the top half of a tarped area will finish first (and quickly because a great deal of the heat from the bottom half moves upwards into the top area). The bottom half will die back, but not fully solarize. At this point, we will slide the tarp down to finish the bottom half (and perhaps start another half section below), or just roll up any unneeded, excess plastic. If you roll the plastic, make sure to roll it **under** the bottom edge. If you roll it up, any rain will pool heavily in the fold of the plastic, making removal far more difficult and creating a place mosquitoes and other pests may multiply.

Shade and sun exposure

Shady spots don't solarize well. The more exposed and open an area, the more effective solarization. If your spot receives less sun because of surrounding woods, hills, buildings, or other features, your solarization will take longer and have to take place during the warmer, sunnier time of year. If shade is an issue, consider trimming trees and other investments to improve the amount of incoming light, not only to improve solarization's success, but also to improve your yields and the types and varieties of plants you can grow.

Timing

The 30–45 days before and 45–60 days after the summer solstice are the ideal time for solarization. The farther you get from the solstice, the longer solarization will take. The closer to the equator you live, the greater the window to use this approach. Those in the far south have as much as six months of the year to solarize, while those in the northern US may have only a month or so to take advantage of this technique.

Weather and temperature

Another factor for successful solarization is cooperative weather. The higher both daytime and nighttime temperatures, the faster and more thorough the final results. The more joined up days of full to mostly sunny conditions (as opposed to cloudy, mostly cloudy, partially cloudy, or rainy), the faster and more thorough the result.

Inconsistent weather can completely derail solarization. Sun then rain then sun then rain can keep the soil from building up sufficient heat to sterilize seeds and destroy plant roots. In such situations, you may reduce and remove annuals, but perennials and plant seeds will generally survive.

Size of solarization space

A final consideration with solarization is the size of the area you plan to solarize. One reason studies and field trials have such mixed results with solarization is not just location and timing, but the size of the trial plots. Small plots are much harder to solarize effectively than larger ones. Many studies and trials I have seen use rather small plots—10x10 or less—to test solarization's effectiveness. Such small spaces don't heat up as quickly or thoroughly as larger plots, especially the outer 2–3 feet on the sides. The earth is a massive thermal buffer. So, the smaller the space, the harder it is to capture enough energy to offset the earth's natural ambient ground temperature buffering effect. If possible, stick with a 20x30 foot or larger plot for best results.

If Solarization Works, Why are so Many Studies so Inconsistent with the Results?

There are many studies on solarization. The effectiveness across studies varies widely. Why? It relates back to the factors listed above. Some studies and field trials are done at poor times of the year or don't take into account and adjust for the the issues I list above. Others are just in locations that make successful solarization far more difficult, regardless of the timing. If you want solarization to work wonders for your weed problems, you need to learn to account for and adjust, and also realize its limits given your location. If you do, solarization success will soon be yours, or you will instead move on to and invest in other, better approaches for your situation!

How Do I Know When Solarization is Successful?

There are a few ways to be sure that your solarization was successful.

First, any solarization done near the summer solstice with little to no rainy or cloudy days and normal or elevated day and night time temperatures will succeed in as little as 10 days. Sometimes it is less, but 10 days is a safe estimate. If you have a nice stretch of weather, the soil was moistened, and the plastic was placed tight against the ground with the edges properly buried, you can be assured that it worked.

Second, you can use one or more thermometers placed under the plastic to check on daytime soil temperatures. After two to three consecutive days with readings over 120 to 130 degrees, you are good to pull the plastic.

Also note, solarization works two ways. First, hitting a sufficiently high temperature for a short period of time will kill weeds and reduce large numbers of seeds and pests in the soil. Also, repeatedly hitting lower temperatures a few days in a row will do the same and sometimes even better than a single high temperature spike. Even imperfect solarization that only reduces and removes surface weeds and seeds will make your garden a great deal easier, especially if you don't follow it with tillage or other types of soil disturbance.

We will often solarize, transplant, then mulch. This creates ideal conditions for transplants in our experience, especially if late April or early May weather allows us to use solarization to also warm up the soil more rapidly for warm season transplants. Once the transplants are established, we will companion plant or sow an understory if and when appropriate to go with the main planting, or for appropriate plants, mulch to reduce any follow up weeding.

Strip Solarization and Partial Solarization

In some beds, I take a lazy approach to solarization, especially in our raised, intensive growing spaces. Instead of burying the plastic I merely strip solarize beds in between plantings to remove shallow rooted grasses, unwanted volunteer plants, and other summer weeds. This also knocks back clovers and other perennials. I then transplant and sometimes also re-mulch the beds. With these perennials, it often doesn't fully kill them, so they will bounce back in two to four weeks, becoming a nice companion planting or understory after the transplants are established. This approach has so far been completely successful in keeping the beds weed free through the fall. The beds are also nicely ready come fall for cover cropping.

I especially like this approach following garlic, lettuce, carrots, cabbage, broccoli, and other early season crops. Often, these have a nice understory of clover, lamb's quarter, or other plants mixed in with the main crop. As we empty these beds, the solarization takes care of any remaining vegetation long before it goes to seed, along with helping eliminate pests and pest eggs from the previous planting that, since stuff was just pulled, are still in the top few inches of the soil. Since many of the above crops' pests go to ground directly underneath their host plants, solarization is a simple way to help break their reproductive cycle each season without chemicals or tillage required.

Note, this approach doesn't reduce the soil seed bank significantly, though it is very effective against any seeds in the top few inches of soil. Instead, it allows us to knock back unwanted plant growth and some pest populations to provide space for fast growing transplants into otherwise undisturbed beds. Since we are not tilling, save through the action of cover crops, we don't have to worry about bringing new weed seeds to the surface, so the soil seed bank isn't a concern.

Cultivation Post Solarization

If you are cultivating, you must be exceptionally careful to not turn up untreated soil post solarization, or you will undo all your effort. Thus, you need to be fairly certain on the depth your solarization achieved and the depth your equipment is going to turn up. It is best to avoid cultivation post solarization. If you need to aerate post solarization or otherwise loosen the soil, consider using a broadfork or similar tool that doesn't require any soil disturbance.

Solarization, Erosion, and Slopes

Solarization is an especially helpful technique to use on sloping growing spaces. Since it leaves all the root matter in the ground, the soil is still well protected post solarization from wind, rain, and erosion. We just pulled a spot from solarization to start planting seed potatoes into. In the middle of the transition, about an inch of rain fell in thirty minutes. If we had tilled or otherwise worked the soil in that space, the rain would have led to catastrophic erosion. Instead, everything held nicely, and the solarization also resulted in better water penetration and retention for planting. As mentioned above, the only drawback to slopes is the lower rate of effectiveness on the low side of the tarp, which sometimes necessitates a staggered approach.

Incorporation into Growing Season

Solarization's biggest drawback is timing. The best time to deploy this tactic is also the height of growing season in most of the United States. How can you not disrupt your growing schedule and still take advantage of one of the most effective weed control methods?

1. Season extension

What makes solarization possible for us is season extension, or what a fellow grower calls "pushing the zone." Planting rules are mostly geared towards amateur growers who need simple, no risk approaches to gardening. They are rules that want to be broken. What if instead of planting potatoes in May, you could be harvesting them? What if instead of putting out lettuces in May, you were already on your twenty fifth day of salad?

There are many ways to push the zone—using low tunnels, floating row cover, transplants and starts, planting in late fall and overwintering in the field, and using varieties that are more heat or cold tolerant. The list of ways to grow more food for more of the year is pretty extensive. Such methods then free up time and space around the solstice to catch your breath and knock back weeds at the same time. I personally love solarizing while my family and I are at the beach. I don't love long hours of field work in the mid to late Kentucky summer. By that point of the year, I want to do a small amount of weeding, a great deal of harvesting, and a fair bit of swimming. So, we manage our growing spaces and schedule accordingly.

2. Strip solarization

If you don't have space to do very large areas at a time with solarization, you can "strip solarize" beds during the middle of the growing season as they turn over. For instance, as garlic is coming out in late May or June, but before you drop in sweet potatoes slips, if weather permits and the plot is in need, solarize it. Or as you harvest the last of your cabbage, take a week to knock back any weeds and seeds before putting out your peppers. This is especially useful for those with limited growing space or shorter seasons who cannot set aside their valuable growing space for even just a week or so, since it is already so limited or so short.

Super Powered Solarization: Biomass Incorporation

A few farms have taken solarization to an entirely new level by incorporating compostable materials into the soil before solarizing. This allows the temperature to increase rapidly and to levels traditional solarization could never achieve—160 or more degrees. At these temperatures, solarization annihilates weeds of any and all kinds, including deep rooted perennials, as well as radically reducing the soil seed bank. Nematodes, pathogens, and other problematic things are also removed. Unlike regular solarization, which generally will infiltrate the soil to around six inches or so of depth at best, solarization plus biomass incorporation can create sufficient heat up to 36 inches deep in the soil.

The technique involves opening up the soil via tillage or other mechanized means to around 12–36 inches deep. Then, you incorporate materials that will create thermophilic compost conditions (composting at high temperatures because of the heat generated by bacterial decomposition). Solarization tarps are applied after the material is incorporated into the soil. Moisture is added as needed, with a heavy watering usually following the original adding of the compostable materials. After five or so days of composting, the soil is checked, and if needed, more water is added.

This process shows great promise, especially when putting in perennials such as orchards in areas where the soil quality is poor, plagued by problematic pests or diseases such as nematodes, or in need of significant improvement and amendment. While generally I am not a fan of tillage and machinery, this is one technique where, if done properly, the amount of soil improvement and long term benefits the system will generate makes it completely worthwhile.

The drawbacks? This technique requires heavy equipment and a large amount of biomass to incorporate. How large an amount? One to two thousand pounds of material for every thousand or so square feet. An acre of land will take many tons of material. You quickly see why this method is especially useful for quickly improving soil quality, since the importation of such a large amount of biomass brings with it many other benefits for needy, poor soils.

Biosolarization is more difficult in soils that are already nutrient laden, as you will need to choose your source of biomass with great care so as to not cause nutrient imbalances in the soil. Soil tests are just one important part of successfully planning a biosolarization project, but one you cannot afford to neglect.

Summary: How to Solarize

- **Prep Area:** Mow space thoroughly—plastic should be as close to the ground as possible. Any woody debris, sticks, or similar material that may puncture the plastic should be removed.
- **Water Area:** Ensure adequate soil moisture by either timing tarp placement to after moderate rain or by watering the space.
- **Dig Trench:** Dig a six inch deep, six inch wide trench on all sides of the area. If your solarization plastic is 30x30, the trenches should be dug at 29x29.
- **Apply and secure tarp:** lay the tarp over the area and bury the edges in the trenches. It is best to do this on a day with little to no wind, especially if you are using a large (over a few hundred square feet) tarp. If it is windy, keep some sand bags on hand to help keep the tarp in place until the edges are buried.
- **Sit and Wait:** Successful solarization generally takes about 10–14 days.
- **Remove tarp, re-inoculate and replant:** Have plants, inputs, and amendments ready to go immediately post solarization. Also have irrigation options ready in case the weather does not cooperate. Remember, for as much of the year as possible, we want roots below and shoots above the ground. Solarization is a brief pause or break in this all important cycle.

14

Occultation: One Tarp to Rule Them All

If solarization ramps up the heat to bring about the ruin of weeds, occultation does the opposite. It seeks to gently warm an area to trick seeds into germination, only to then suffocate them under the low air and no light environment the occultation tarp creates. It is death by asphyxiation plus starvation for unwanted plant species. When done properly, it is very effective. It is not without drawbacks—there are a number of grass and weed species that occultation may make worse.

Unlike solarization, which has to happen near the summer solstice, occultation can happen almost any time, but is especially common to use in late fall and late winter/early spring, happening at a time similar to forced germination. In the far north or Canada, it may not work during winter at all.

Occultation is the opposite of solarization in many ways. Instead of seeking to drive up soil temperatures to the point of weed and seed destruction through maximizing incoming solar gain and concentrating in the top layers of the soil, occultation seeks to cut off light, air, and other resources from the soil, *while still encouraging weeds to germinate*. Basically, it is akin to smothering young seedlings, getting them to germinate so that they can then die from lack of air and light.

Occultation is slightly simpler than solarization in some ways. The preparation of a site for occultation is identical to the preparation for solarization. The difference? Slope, shade, and other factors matter far less, if at all. Also, unlike the variable time frame for success that solarization creates, occultation takes roughly the same amount of time regardless of the time of year the technique is used. Generally, 6–8 weeks are needed for occultation to work.

Unlike solarization, occultation uses dark, heavy tarps laid over the soil rather than clear plastic. These are secured in a similar manner to solarization, either via trenching or sandbags. While occultation tarps are generally heavier duty than solarization plastic, I still don't recommend using concrete blocks or other materials to secure them since you may damage the tarp. Soil moisture still matters, so watering may be necessary before applying your tarp. The soil should be moist, neither dry nor waterlogged.

Occultation is not as thorough or as effective as solarization, especially against perennials. It will weaken but rarely kill them. It has the benefit of being something that can be done during off season, especially in mid-latitude areas where warm streaks and adequate moisture punctuate the long winter, creating perfect windows to encourage weed germination. Occultation pairs well with other techniques, such as flame weeding, chicken incorporation, or light cultivation, to kill the germinated plants more quickly and tie up bed space for shorter periods of time.

What Do You Need to Occultate?

Usually, growers use heavy grade tarps—most often silage, sometimes billboard, or similar. The tarp should be about 10% larger than the area you plan to occultate. So if you want to do a 30x40 foot space, I would use a tarp that was 35x45 feet to ensure that the edges are effectively treated as well. Otherwise, plants may grow sideways out from under the tarp to access light and air, leaving the edges still quite plant infested and weedy.

A word or two of caution about vinyl billboard tarps

Some people recommend using old vinyl billboard signs to occultate. The reasons are mainly financial—they are very, very large (often around 30x50 feet) and are also very inexpensive. In my area, they are available on numerous websites (Craigslist, Facebook marketplace) for as little as $20–50 depending on the size—pocket change per square foot pricing! That works out to about three to seven cents per square foot.

Unfortunately, they present a real problem for soil contamination through both the vinyl itself and the inks and dyes applied to it. A few researchers hope to look into this issue, but also felt for this reason alone caution was warranted. Further, when they degrade—usually in two or so years in our experience—they shred into innumerable tiny pieces that spread throughout your homestead, farm, and ecosystem. They create an incredibly difficult to deal with mess unless you remove and dispose of them before they become brittle and began to break down.

I also wonder if an organic certifier would approve this method given the tarps' ability to leach chemicals. A number of growers stated that their certifier does not permit their use. Again, studies are needed to know exactly what is in these and what leaches out when laid in contact with the ground. Until then, silage or similar tarps are preferred and recommended.

To Cultivate or not to Cultivate, That is the Question!

Cultivation—the light working of the top half to one inch of soil—is often used pre-occultation and forced germination to increase their effectiveness. By cultivating, you bring up seeds in the top inch or so of soil to increase the number of weeds that germinate. Depending on your soil and a few other factors, a pass or two with a cultivating tool, which can be something as simple as a rake, is often worthwhile before you put your tarp down.

How to Occultate

- **Prep Area:** Any woody debris, sticks, or similar material should be removed or reduced via mowing. Ensure adequate soil moisture by either timing tarp placement to after moderate rain or by watering the space.
- **Light cultivation:** Optional, but for many situations will improve results.
- **Apply tarp:** lay the tarp over the area you plan to occultate. It is best to do this on a day with little to no wind, especially if you are using a large (over a few hundred square feet) tarp.
- **Secure tarp:** There are many ways to secure the tarp. Like with solarization, you can bury the edges. In more northernly locations and cooler times of the year, this may improve your results. Some growers will use stones, cinder blocks or similar materials to secure the tarp. The one concern with such materials is that they can cause puncture or rip the tarp. My preference is sandbags or a similar non abrasive weight for this reason.
- **Sit and Wait:** Successful occultation takes about 30–45 days. Field studies appear to show that, more than location, it is the length of tarping that matters most for success. Further north, weather and other factors may also play a role.

Solarization vs. Occultation

Both solarization and occultation are excellent ways to reduce weeds. How do you decide which to use? Each grower will need to decide based on their goals, situation, and timing. Solarization is better than occultation on a number of levels, but in most locations, the need to do it during the height of growing season makes it much harder to fit into some rotations and schedules. If you are really far north, losing a few weeks of prime growing time to solarization may not make sense— stick with occultation and other methods.

For those with longer seasons, especially ones that allow for multiple plantings in the same bed, solarization between plantings is exceptionally effective during the heart of summer. At the very least, taking a few days to strip solarize, especially when the weather won't permit or promote good planting or transplanting anyway—makes excellent sense. What types of conditions don't make for good transplanting? Full sun, warm temperatures, and no rain forecasted—the perfect conditions for solarizing!

Occultation and Crop Germination

A final note about occultation. Sometimes, growers will use occultation tarps to help certain early season crops—such as carrots, beets, and a few others—germinate.

This technique requires a fair bit of skill and careful timing, but has a number of benefits. Sometimes, flame weeding is tossed into the mix. First, a bed will be prepped. An occultation tarp will be applied. After a few weeks, the tarp will be lifted and the bed flame weeded to remove the first round of emergent weeds. Then, the bed will be planted to carrots or another, slow to germinate crop. The bed will be watered and the tarp will be reapplied. Then, again in a week or so, but before the carrots have germinated, the tarp will be pulled and the bed re-flamed. The tarp is applied one last time and once the carrots have germinated, removed permanently.

Such an approach increases up front labor, but decreases weed load substantially while not only not delaying planting, but allowing some crops to get a head start under the protection and warm environment the tarp creates. It can also significantly improve crop germination rates, especially for more difficult to deal with plants.

Part Four

Concentrated Weed Control

In this part, we will look some weed control methods that are quick and highly effective at killing off weeds at various stages, but require specialized equipment. These methods have a number of advantages over the others outlined above. The biggest are flexibility and speed. occultation, solarization, and forced germination will tie up growing spaces for a few days to a few weeks, but generally take up at least two to four weeks calendar-wise. While a smart grower can time this to minimize disruption, weather and life don't always cooperate. Or, the technique for whatever reason isn't effective or sufficiently effective for a grower's needs and goals.

The next set of tools and techniques we cover tie up a growing space for a few minutes to hours at most. Also, unlike the earlier approaches that take planning and a certain level of right understanding and application, the below take far less skill to use successfully (you will notice this section is a fair bit shorter than the preceding ones!). As long as you operate the equipment according to manufacturer instructions and hit the plants at the right time and stage of growth, you win.

Also, unlike mulches of all kinds—geotextiles, plasticulture, woodchips, hay and the like—these methods don't limit your planting options. You can still use a paperpot or Jang or other rapid planting, transplanting, or seeding tools with the options that we are about to cover. This is why these are very popular among market gardeners and many other growers.

While these are faster and generally, at least physically, easier weed control methods, they are also more expensive. For smaller operations or homesteaders, the current cost of such equipment often makes these options impractical or financially imprudent. Many growers stated that such tools require at least an acre or more in production before they become cost effective to own. For homesteaders and other smaller growers, a group co-owning such tools would possibly make sense. A thousand dollar investment spread over four households that saves a great deal of labor and improves your yields is a pretty easy investment, as long as the co-owners are all trustworthy.

The other big drawback to these methods? Timing is critical. With solarization, if a space gets a bit overrun, you can mow it down and then solarize anyway, even taking care of stuff that went to seed and the seeds at the same time. With occultation, you can toss the tarp down at almost anytime so long as, like solarization, the ground is prepped and cleared. With flaming or steaming, a space must be hit at the right time to ensure effectiveness. Too early or too late will result in significant weed pressure later. A few days early or late just won't do it.

15

Flame Weeding

While solarization and occultation are great tools, they don't always work fully or sometimes you miss the window to make them happen. You walk out and find yourself facing significant weed pressure in a growing bed that needs planted as soon as possible or perhaps in the paths close by. What do you do? Flame weeding is one option. Think of it as deploying concentrated, stored sunshine to scorch weeds into submission.

Flame weeding does not involve burning weeds to ash and dust. Sorry, no reliving your Arachnophobia flamethrower dreams! Instead, properly done, during a brief pass over the plant the heat a flame weeder generates damages its cellular structure. This damage then leads to the plant's eventual demise in two to four days. Flame weeding works exceptionally well against young annuals. Against perennials or those with strong and deep root systems, it may take multiple passes to kill them, if it does so at all. Generally, flame weeding will only mildly weaken such strong invaders, especially if they are well established.

Flame weeding is an efficient, effective, and relatively low cost method, especially for market and organic growers. It does require careful timing—**it works best on newly emergent weeds**. Once plants are well established, or an area is thickly covered by invaders, the effectiveness drops substantially unless you are willing to flame weed repeatedly or very slowly. This increases the cost per square foot substantially, both in terms of labor and fuel. This is one reason why flame weeding is generally used with occultation. Occultation allows a grower to force the germination of many young plants all at once, which they then knock back via flame weeding.

If your growing space is small—say some raised beds or a thousand square feet or less—there are a few hand flame weeders available. If you growing space is very large, especially if you are at an acre or more, then you are going to want to check out models specifically designed for market growers. These generally involve multiple flame heads mounted on a rolling frame that allows quick, single passes over standard bed sizes.

Another benefit of hand flame weeding models is the ability to use them against certain pests. For instance, a few growers I know will flame leaves overrun by squash bugs or covered in their eggs. This ensures 100% egg eradication and high levels of bug deaths as well with minimal plant damage.

Flame Weeding Cost Estimates

One reason flame weeding is popular is because it is inexpensive, save the initial equipment. You can generally do 1/3 to 1/2 of an acre on a single 20 pound (4.7 gallon) propane tank. While costs vary, a good estimate is around $4.00/gallon for propane. So, you are looking at around $20 per 1/3 acre of flaming (about 15,000 square feet).

There are a few factors that impact the cost. First, poor or improper grading and bed prep. Bumpy, rocky, or uneven ground makes you go slower and can also reduce effectiveness, requiring additional passes. So make sure that your beds are well formed and that the ground is even and properly shaped. Second, small propane tanks cost more than larger ones. If your scale justifies the investment, you can purchase larger tanks and the necessary adapters so that you can refill your smaller tanks yourself. Given the already low cost to flame weed with the 20 pound tank, most growers opt for the convenience of just returning or refilling those.

Safely Flame Weeding

Flame weeding does have a few risks. First, fire. Whenever flame weeding, make sure to have a hose or similar ready supply of water handy. Don't flame weed on dry, windy days! If your area is in drought conditions, take additional precautions, such as irrigating an area the day before flaming. This is doubly true if you have lingering mulch/crop residue that may create embers that then get carried by the wind. Speaking of mulch, you will need to rake back/remove mulch, and if the mulch is very dry, exercise caution in when and how you use a flame weeding setup.

Also note, flame weeders don't play nice with landscape fabric, irrigation equipment like drip tape, or anything else plastic or flammable. So make sure you have fully cleared areas you plan to flame weed before you get rolling along. Many a grower has damaged tools and infrastructure by not first clearing their growing space properly.

16

Steaming and Boiling Water

Hot water is dangerous. But most people don't realize that steam can be as or even more dangerous. Burns from steam are actually more damaging to the skin than those from hot water! That same steam power is yet another way to use heat to help eliminate weeds. In a sense, steaming is very similar to solarization, just instead of using current solar energy, it uses stored solar energy to heat up water to create steam that is then forced a few inches deep into the soil.

When done properly, steaming has a high rate of effectiveness—you are looking at a 95–100% reduction in weeds and weed seeds. This sets steaming apart from flaming—with flaming, there is no draw down in the soil seed bank beyond what has germinated. With steaming, you not only remove any germinated plants, you also take out 90% of the seeds in the top three to four inches of soil. Also, unlike flaming you can cause significant damage to perennials. Young, newly emergent perennials may not survive proper steaming at all, while established ones may suffer significant damage. Also, studies have shown that steaming appears to benefit the plantings that follow—improving growth rate, yields, disease resistance, and more.

While steaming is very effective, it has a number of drawbacks. First, it is slow. It takes many minutes to treat each section of soil and each section may only be about 100–200 or so square feet in size. So you are looking at 30 minutes to treat 1000 square feet. That is about five to ten hours per half acre, a sizeable time investment.

Second, currently it requires highly specialized and expensive equipment. This is one reason flame weeding is so popular even if it is not nearly as effective. The entry cost for a thirty inch flame weeder is under $1,000 and you can flame a hundred foot row in just in ten or so minutes. While there are some small and inexpensive steam weeders, they only do very small areas (a few square inches) at a time. Reviews also suggest that these options are generally made poorly and from low quality materials. They won't hold up for any kind of intensive, repetitive garden, homestead, or farm work. Mid-grade units are most likely out of reach for the majority of growers—these currently are just under ten thousand dollars!

While billed as an option for hobby farms by the makers, unless it is Bruce Wayne or some other well-to-do person's hobby farm, I don't expect to see too many of my friends plunking down that amount of cash just to control a few weeds. These units are very economical and effective in urban settings, though, and you may see them replacing herbicides in parks, schools, and other places in forward thinking cities, colleges, parks, and some landscaping companies. I could also see if the prices come down a bit more, a group of homesteaders or farmers co-owning a unit to make it more economical.

Handheld steam weeders do have one significant side benefit—you can also use them for pest control in a wide range of other situations and scenarios. They are an especially appropriate option for taking care of a number of aggressive, stinging pests such as hornets and wasps. A steam weeder serves as a great alternative to chemical sprays and other controls that have risks to both people and beneficial insect populations.

Boiling Water

On a limited scale, especially in raised beds or for treating small, problematic spots, you can make and use boiling water. Why is boiling water not generally employed? It is both hard to make in quantity, heavy to move, and dangerous to apply. As with steaming, you should wear protective clothing (long pants and sleeves, waterproof boots and the like) and apply the boiling water (over 200 degrees is needed for best results) carefully. Also note, boiling water can easily damage nearby plants.

17

Animal Incorporation

I would be remiss not to mention the use of animals to help reduce weed problems. Animals are often used in conjunction with cover crops, since one way to gain additional value from a cover crop is to grow it not only to protect and improve your soil, but also to provide high quality food for animals on your farm or homestead.

Certain areas, such as semi-sturdy perennials like berries and other plants, don't play well with some approaches outlined above for weed control. While mulching works well for perennials, especially wood based mulches, weeding these areas is often difficult and time consuming, along with posing significant danger to the plants. Animals make excellent workers to help deweed such areas. No animal is better adapted to this task than the lowly chicken. Equipped with talons that would make the most fearsome weed quake, a love of green matter and plant seed, and an insatiable desire to lightly shred the ground in search of food, chickens are excellent weeders. Also, their high nitrogen manure, as long as your soil needs it and the additional phosphorus and potassium won't cause problems, can help "burn" out unwanted plants.

Chickens can also help reduce certain pests substantially at the same time. In some other countries, ducks are used extensively for pest control in vineyards and orchards for this reason. Think of fowl as nature's free lightweight debuggers and tillers that also give you eggs and meat in return for their labor instead of requiring gas and time to operate. One reason so many growers struggle with problems in berry patches and orchards is that we have removed one of nature's best forms of pest control—various animal species like chickens, ducks, and turkeys.

Weeding with chickens or other avian species takes some skill to master. We generally follow these rules:

1. High impact for short time—the greater the number of chickens and the smaller the space, the shorter the window we give them to do their work.

2. Timed to remove early season weeds and pests—too early and there are no young plants to eat and uproot or emergent pests to eat—too late and some plants are too well established to be deterred and damaged by the chickens.

3. Proper withdrawal so that any manure is dealt with before planting.

Chickens are not the only animal, though, that can help. Historically, pigs have played an important role in clearing fields and preparing ground for subsequent planting. For instance, in the south, before machinery took over harvesting duties on many farms, pigs played clean up crew for peanuts, sweet potatoes, and a host of other crops. Pigs were often deployed in the fall, which helped farmers by providing additional feed for the pigs as they neared butchering, while also helping clean up and fertilizer the fields for next year's spring planting.

Pigs require even more care and skill to use without creating problems compared to chickens. For instance, their desire to root and dig can turn up just as many or more weeds as they tear down. They can leave ground quite uneven and pitted, requiring a great deal of work after their removal to get the ground back into plantable condition. Their presence can also lead to compaction and other problems if they are left in an area too long or at too high a stocking rate. Thus, if you go with pigs, make sure to keep a close eye on the condition of the area you let them work.

In my view, the best way to use pigs is when trying to turn a new or badly overrun area back into annual production. They are an excellent first line of offense to break up compaction, work in added materials (like coffee grounds, composts, and the like) and knock back many types of weeds. Once the pigs are removed, you can then treat the area with one of the other methods we have discussed.

Using animals also has two other areas of concern that growers must consider—food safety and fertility.

Animal Incorporation and Food Safety

Note that for market growers or anyone selling any kind of produce, using chickens or other animals for pest and weed control comes with significant limitations. The Food Safety Modernization Act has strict rules regarding animal manures and crop production. The basic rule of thumb is you can't have animals in actively growing vegetable spaces.

The limitations are tied to the risk of pathogens in animal manures that may find their way on or into produce. Produce that is consumed raw is especially at risk, such as leafy greens. If you use chickens or any other animal in a growing space, the most recent rule iteration required 180 days before harvesting.

Animal Incorporation and Fertility

A final note on using animals in growing spaces. Depending on your nutrient levels and the number of animals you plan to deploy, you need to exercise caution to ensure that the animal manures don't create nutrient imbalances. Phosphorus (P) and potassium (K), which chicken and many other manures are high in, are of special concern.

In my many years now of doing consulting work with growers and homesteaders, the above is a repeated issue that I encounter. Soil test after soil test shows elevated to skyrocketing levels of P and K from repeated animal exposure or over reliance on animal manures or animal heavy composts. Animal manures contain far too little nitrogen for the amount of other nutrients they often contain. The nutrients tend to build up in just a few years in the soil, negatively impacting plant health and yields. At some point, if not caught early enough, it can create an incredibly difficult condition to correct—in many soil types, getting excess nutrients out is much harder than getting them in.

This is also a problem if you depend primarily on animal manures for the bulk of your fertility. Annual soil tests, cover cropping, and other tools are absolutely necessary to keep your soil in balance and keep your growing spaces going well for the long haul. Don't neglect to get soil tests done, especially if you are considering using animals to help control weed issues.

Keeping Animals In and Out: Fencing and Row Cover

What if you have certain beds or spaces in production, such as over-wintered garlic or early greens? How do you protect these plantings while still letting chickens or another animal take care of early season weeds and pests in nearby places?

Portable electronet style fencing is the simplest solution. Such fencing can be used to protect small plots, or as cross fencing to divide a larger plot into forageable areas. In our experience, it doesn't even need electrified if we are using it to keep chickens **out** of a small space or merely as a boundary fence between two areas. Another option, especially if your chickens are flighty, is to make a temporary cross-fence using 2x4 welded wire or similar material on t-posts. Such a fence is even less likely to have a bird breakthrough and is still fairly simple to install and remove.

A second way to keep a crop safe is with floating row cover. For garlic or similar beds we can just lay the floating row cover directly over the plants and the chickens generally just ignore such plots or spaces. This allows the chickens a great deal of freedom to roam and clean up the rest of a growing space, while protecting a few key overwintered, early spring, or late fall plantings.

Part Five

It's the End of the Weeds as We Know It

So, we are almost done with weeds! At least, I hope, after finishing up, you will be done having to spend so much time fighting weeds and can get back to more enjoyable and productive gardening and other pursuits than punishing yourself each growing season.

18

Understanding How Tools Impact Techniques and Tactics

You can think of growing food as a choose your own adventure book. You come to a point in the story and get to make a decision. That decision requires you to choose between two or three different paths. The path you take, the decision you make, directly impacts what follows.

So it is with growing food. Take how you get plants in the ground. You can do direct seed, do transplants, or use a paperpot or similar transplanter, or Jang or similar seeder. It is a choice, a fork in the road. If you go with transplants, you have one set of weed control options, such as using geotextiles or mulches to transplant into. If you go with the paperpot, geotextiles are out, so, you have to choose a different method to deal with weeds, like cultivation for some crops, mulches for others.

Or, you can do direct seed, but that doesn't work with geotextiles, or for many small seeded plants, organic mulches. If you direct seed, how will you control weeds? Occultation before and light cultivation after? Again, each decision impacts others and determines what will come next during your growing season.

Also, your choice of how you seed or get plants in the ground isn't the only factor. The type of plant matters as well. Some plants do well with deep, organic mulches, others don't. Below, I have laid out a number of technique flows used by our homestead and by many other farms and homesteads. This gives you some insight into how different approaches tie together over the course of a season, and how you might plan plan out your approach.

Examples of common growing technique work flows

- Fall cover crop → Spring mow/flail mow → Allow 1–2 week breakdown → Transplant cabbage, broccoli or similar cool season crops → Add organic mulches if needed/desired (straw or small size, aged wood chips) → Harvest cool season crops → Sow summer cover crop → Mow as needed → Late summer kill via solarization → Plant cool season crop → Fallow over winter

- Forced germination or occultation → (early to mid spring) flame weeding, steam weeding, or light cultivation → Direct seed or transplanting (hand, paperpot, etc.) → Mulch or continued cultivation or hand weeding

- Start transplants or make plans for purchase → Install ag plastic, IRT, or geotextile with drip irrigation → Transplant into holes → Harvest as appropriate → Removal of plastic, IRT, and sometimes geotextile at end of season along with drip irrigation removal

- Start transplants or make plans for purchase → Knock down cover crop if needed → Transplant into cover crop mulch as weather permits → Harvest as appropriate → If weather/season permits, do 2nd croppings → In fall, sow cover crops to establish before winter

- Occultation → Cabbage, onions, or similar crops → Selectively weed, allowing clover or other wanted companion plants to take up space or sow a clover companion crop → Harvest → Mow, clean, and strip solarize → Transplant and re-mulch or reseed

- Occultation → Carrots, lettuce, cabbage, or similar crops → Intercrop radishes → Harvest → Mow, clean, solarize or reoccultate→ Transplant and re-mulch or reseed

- Occultation → Carrots, lettuce, cabbage, or similar crops → Harvest → Mow and clean → Cover crop

- Solarization → Transplant → Mulch → Companion plant or sow understory
- Early season transplants such as brassicas, lettuce, etc. → Harvest → Mow if necessary → Summer cover crop (clover, buckwheat, etc.) → Fall transplant or sowing (carrots, spinach, etc.)

19

Keeping the Weeds Away

One year of seed is seven years of weeds.

—Elliot Coleman

Now that you are winning against weeds, we can move from offense to defense. How do we keep our lovely spaces weed free moving forward, beyond using the techniques and tactics we have already gone over? Remember, a growing space is only one mistake away from the reintroduction of all sorts of unwanted seeds and weeds. In this last section, I want to give some brief thoughts on the most common ways you can accidentally undo all your hard work.

Letting Stuff Go to Seed

It doesn't matter how good your weed management is for 95% of the growing season if you let just a few plants make it to the reproductive phase of their program. A single grass plant can produce 10,000 seeds in a single season. You see where this math is going? Once gone to seed, in just a few days much of your hard work will be undone. Lamb's quarter, pig weed, and many others are also prolific producers of seed. Allowing just a few of a wide variety of plants to seed, especially in windy conditions, can repopulate large sections of a relatively weed free growing space.

This is one reason why it is better to oversee a **smaller** space and do it well than a larger space and do it poorly. Four hundred well managed square feet will outperform and outproduce four thousand square feet of weed and pest overran plants. On our property, 1200 square feet of high tunnel space yields more than over five thousand square feet of field space. It isn't just the season extending properties of the high tunnel—it is the intensive management and attention it receives that makes it so productive. So, make sure you choose a plot size you can manage well. You will get far more food for far less work and frustration by doing a small space well than a large space poorly.

Compost

Large animal manure based composts, especially horse, cow, and goat, will carry far more weed seed than other types of compost or manures, such as those from bats, rabbits, chickens, and similar animals. Animals that eat full sized grasses and weeds and whose digestive systems do not grind down material will poop out more viable, intact grass and weed seeds.

It is much harder to compost animal manures properly to achieve a 95% or greater sterilization of weed seeds than most people realize. Also, many compost piles are not protected from seed exposure after the composting process is completed. So, even if a pile was thoroughly and properly composted, wind, weather, and poor protection of the finished piles may mean that the piles get repopulated with many unwanted plants.

Years ago, I saw this problem first-hand at a friend's farm. They raise horses and cattle, and the manure and bedding from both is then used in the vegetable production side of the farm. The compost piles were built and kept along pasture edges, and after turning, often sat unprotected for weeks or months. By the time they would start collecting compost to use for produce, the piles were already starting to turn back into pasture! This particular farm ended up having some significant weed issues that cost them large amounts of money a number of seasons in a row!

If I were to purchase off-farm compost, I would:

1. Check to see how they make it. Does it get turned properly and reach sufficient temperatures to sterilize almost all weed seeds? How weed free are the areas around the compost piles? How far from pasture or similar high seed areas are the piles? Are the piles downwind from weedy spots? Do any walls or windbreaks provide protection from reseeding? Are finished piles tarped?

2. Take samples and test for weed and seed load before purchase—spread the compost an inch or so deep in a warm, sunny place and apply water. If it is an especially rich compost, I may cut it with a sterile medium like potting mix to ensure a fair trial.

3. Use forced germination, solarization, or occultation before applying compost to reduce and remove any remaining weed seeds, especially if 1 or 2 show that this is necessary or prudent.

For a number of years, I would purchase dump truck loads of cow manure from the local stockyard's disposal service. It was incredibly affordable at the time—$30 dollars for ten or so tons of material delivered right to our farm. The problem? It was weed heaven. The material was poorly composted if at all. The piles were exposed to all sorts of weed seeds from the surrounding environment that was overgrown and overrun by brush, invasive trees and plants, weeds, and grasses. Also, sometimes the animals were bedded on hay instead of straw, and either way lots of hay was trampled down into bedding, adding even more seeds to the mix. In our first few years, many of the worst weeds that took root in our growing spaces came from this compost. Our infestation of pigweed came courtesy of this low cost compost. If you have dealt with pigweed or a similar noxious plant, you quickly realize just how costly some low quality, low cost compost can be!

To make this material suitable for any use other than pasture, you can take a pile of it, level it slightly to about 2–4 inches deep, add water if needed, and then use the appropriate approach for the time of year to lessen the weed load—solarization, occultation, etc. You may need to repeat the process twice if necessary. Added work? Yes. Better than adding tens of thousands of viable weed seeds to your growing spaces? Absolutely! Even better? Just avoiding such weed-laden materials to begin with!

Equipment, Tools, and Clothing

Some people use four wheelers or other small machines to mosey around their farm. After dashing through woods or pasture or other spots, they pull up into their growing spaces…importing all sorts of unwanted plant matter and seeds in the process.

Or you go walking in the morning, and decide to stroll the pasture or across the lawn before setting foot in the high tunnel. The lovely morning dew that coats your boots allows all sorts of seeds to catch a ride as well. As you work in the high tunnel, the dew dries and the seeds drop into nice, fertile ground, courtesy of your spread-the-weed kindness. Or have you ever, after working around your homestead, walked inside and discovered that your boots and pants are impregnated by all sorts of seeds and burrs? Do you put those same clothes back on the next day when you go out to work in your garden?

Or perhaps you cultivated a weedy area in the garden with some tool, where stuff had gone to seed, only to neglect to wash the tool thoroughly before moving it to a new spot for more work. The weeds catch a free ride to virgin space, ready to get back to work.

Such is how you can easily undo hard weeding work. If you or your equipment or tools have to travel through weedy areas, make sure to decontaminate before you relocate. Change clothes, wash boots, rinse off equipment and tools. A few minutes of cleanup can save you many hours of weed work later.

Dedicated Tools and Equipment When Possible

For a number of techniques we use to control weeds the growing spaces require mowing, either to reduce stubble and other material that may harm plastic or tarps, or to knock back a cover crop or residual plant matter to make space for the next planting or purpose.

To do this work, we use a dedicated lawnmower that we purchased used for $50. Why dedicated? It is almost impossible to clean a mower constantly that is run over grassy and weedy areas of all the seed that builds up in and on it. You will spend hours washing it before you ever get close to removing the compacted, caked, and otherwise every nook and cranny occupied spots seeds and seed heads may stick. Then, the next time you mow, you move these seeds from grassy areas to your growing spaces. So we found it was far less expensive, especially in terms of labor, to have a mower set aside just for garden use, so that we weren't undoing our hard won efforts at reducing seed and weed load by using equipment in non-complementary growing spaces. If it does need cleaned after clearing a seedy spot in the garden, it doesn't have many mowings of built-up detritus and seed mixed in to deal with, so the task is far more manageable and enjoyable. Generally, though, we avoid mowing spots that have gone to seed if at all possible, since it is hard not to further spread the problem. Instead, we will hand weed or scythe and collect the seedy material and relocate it. It helps remind us of why you don't want to let stuff get to this stage in the future!

This applies to many other tools and pieces of equipment if possible. Our garden cart gets a thorough cleaning anytime it is used in grassy areas before it gets moved back into growing spaces. Same with shovels and other hand tools.

If you are using larger equipment, like tractors, think of how much seed you could be adding to your compost areas by accident. You drive out in the dewy morning across the grass, perhaps to move a chicken tractor or bales of hay or some other material. You then decide to turn compost, taking your seed-caked tires into your compost area and adding untold seeds in the process.

Maintain Weed Free Paths and Access Points

Our compost field and garden entrances are kept weed free, generally with mulches and other methods when necessary. This helps keep us from moving weed seeds around and also reduces how careful we have to be to do so. Imagine that your garden is surrounded by grass on all sides and that you have to cross a hundred feet of lawn or pasture before you get to it. There is no way you won't carry weeds and seeds with you. So, provide mulched paths and access points. Think of these as transition spaces, where you go from grass and other places into your hopefully relatively weed free paradise. Such spaces provide a place for you and others to naturally de-weed before entering the growing space proper.

Charts

I hope the above chapters give you a good foundation for getting your weed grumbling under control without a hoe. To help make it easier to understand and apply all this information, we have one more section left—summary charts that cram all that information into an easy to understand, access, and apply format. When you have a question, you can always start here and then if needed, go back to the chapter if you still require more information.

The armory – weapons for controlling weeds

Technique	When?	Effectiveness?	Benefits	Drawbacks
Eat your enemies	Anytime!	Moderate, great way to turn weeding into a time/revenue positive task	Many weeds are more nutritious, often by significant amounts, than modern plants	If you have a large growing space, unless you are a rabbit, you won't be able to eat enough to make a big dent
Forced Germination	Late fall through late winter/early spring, though can be used at anytime	50-80% reduction in weed seed load, may also weaken some deep rooted, perennial and rhizome reproducers. Depending on conditions, can be done multiple times if weather permits.	Supports soil food web, may help promote early season soil warming to allow earlier planting	Amount of reduction may be relatively low, especially for certain persistant, perennial, or otherwise problematic weeds
Solarization	30 days before to 45 days after Summer solstice	95%+ for both weeds and weed seeds, also may knock back or eliminate some perennial and rhizome reproducers	Most effective method to remove both weeds and weed seeds. Also helps with soil borne pathogens and pests.	Ties up space during prime growing season. Cooperation of weather is critical.
Cover Crops	Anytime, depending on purpose and goal	95%+ suppression with proper cover crop mixes	Greatly improves soil health, confuses pests, attracts pollinators	Timing is critical, not applicable or usable in all situations or growing settings
Occultation	Late fall through late winter/early spring	Excellent reduction in weed seed load, may also weaken some deep rooted, perennial and rhizome reproducers	Promotes soil warming, possibly assisting earlier planting, provides some food for soil food web	Concerns over chemicals in occultation tarps, creates environment for certain rodent type pests to proliferate
Companion planting	Anytime during growing season	Can reduce weeding by up to 75% while also improving plant health, yields, and providing protection from pests	Improves your main plants health and yields. Attracts and provides habitat for many beneficial garden creatures.	Timing is critical - will not work well on plants over 3-4 inches with well established root and leaf systems
Bury the dead: mulching!	Before weeds are well estalished	80-95% reduction in weed germination.	Reduces watering, increases soil formation, protects soil from erosion, wind, rain, and other types of damage. Probably the single most beneficial thing you can to do a growing space soil health wise!	If not broken down by end of winter, may delay spring planting by keeping soil moist and cold. Many seeders and transplanters don't work well with deep mulches.
Scorch the earth: Flame Weeding	Anytime before main crop germinates or is transplanted	95% +/- for early season weed reduction if done properly.	May also help eliminate some surface pests	Timing is critical - will not work well on plants over 3-4 inches with well established root and leaf systems. Cannot be used once main plants have germinated or been transplanted
Get steamed: Water warfare	Anytime before main crop is SEEDED or is transplanted	95% +/- for early season weed reduction, may also help with soil borne pests and pathogens	Depending on setup, excellent against some soil pathogens and pests	Requires specialized equipment
Organic chemicals	Depends on chemical and care of application	Depends on type of weed, how well established and other factors		Cost, possible negative impact on soil health

Timing Guide

The below shows when we commonly use particular techniques. You will need to adjust for your location, climate, and other factors.

We are zone 6B.

January	February	March	April	May	June	July	August	September	October	November	December
		Equinox 20th			Solstice 21st			Equinox 22nd			Solstice 21st

Solarization

Occultation

Flame, steam, mow, handweed, light cultivation

Forced Germination

Seed and establish summer cover crops

Seed and establish fall (frost killed) and winter cover crops

Organic and Inorganic Mulches Applied

Start spring and summer transplants

Transplant starts

Start fall transplants

Note, occultation can be used all season, including over winter. Especially if you are turning over a bed that has light weed load into the growing season, say from an early crop

Cost Comparison

Tree Based Mulches

	Durability	Depth to apply	Cost per square foot	Cost per square foot per year	Notes
Pine Straw (Needles)	1-2 years	3-6 inches	Collection costs only		
Leaves	3-6 months	3-6 inches			
Bark Mulch	2-3 years	3-4 inches	.04-.08	.02-.04	Make sure it is sufficiently chipped - large pieces will not break down properly and be difficult to work with and around
Ramial Chipped Wood	3-6 months	3-6 inches	Most likely will need to make yourself		Generally, hard to find and source, especially in most parts of the US
Woods chip, small or fine	8-12 months	3-6 inches	.04-.08	.04-.08	For wood chips, I am estimating a price of $5.00-$10 per cubic yard, which covers approximately 80 square feet at 4 inches deep
Wood chips, medium	12-18 months	3-6 inches	.04-.08	.04-.06	
Wood chips, large	16-24 months	3-6 inches	.04-.08	.02-.04	

Grass and Plant Based Mulches

	Durability	Depth to apply	Cost per square foot	Cost per square foot per year	Notes
Straw	6-9months	6-12 inches	.03-.10	.03-.10	Herbicide and weed/grass seed risk
Hay (note, particular species are more durable and higher in fertility than others, such as alfalfa, while often being lower in weed seed load)	4-8 months	6-12 inches	.06-.15	.06-.15	Herbicide and weed/grass seed risk
Grass clipping	1-2 months	2-4 inches	Collection costs only	N/A	Herbicide and weed/grass seed risk
Cover Crops, crimped and rolled or flail mowed	3-6 months	Varies	Depends on seed costs, types used	N/A	May require specialized equipment to plant into, especially at larger scale

Man-Made Mulches

	Durability	Depth to apply	Cost per square foot	Cost per square foot per year	Notes
Black or white plastic, non-biodegradble	One season	N/A	.02-.08	.02-.08	Does not include cost of irrigation/drip tape
Biodegradable plastic mulch	One season	N/A	.03-.06	.03-.06	Does not include cost of irrigation/drip tape
Landscape Fabric	3-5 years, if removed or protected over winter	N/A	.04-.12	.01-.04	Does not include cost of irrigation/drip tape
Metal Mulch	10+ years	N/A	.20-1.00	.02-.10	Only suitable for paths and similar places
Heavy Duty Ground Cover Fabric	7-12 years	N/A	.19-.24	.02-.04	Does not include cost of irrigation/drip tape

John's Big Guide to Organic Mulches
Tree Based Mulches

	C/N Ratio	Durability	Thickness to apply	Cost per square foot	Desirability as garden mulch	Do's and Don'ts	
Sawdust	300–500:1	1–2 years	–		4	Generally, not appropriate for growing spaces, good as animal bedding in a mixed bedding system or in moderate amounts in compost making	With both sawdust and wood shavings, be certain they do not contain fake wood/laminates, treated wood or lumber, painted wood, or any other such contaminants. They need to be pure, 100% real wood
Wood Shavings	300–500:1	3–9 months	–		5		
Pine Straw (Dried pine needles)	80:1	1–2 years	3–6 inches		8	Resists wind better than leaf, straw, and hay, weed free, pest deterrent, useful material for birds, easy to apply, generally must purchase	Will not acidify the soil. Even fresh needles have only a very weak acidifying impact on soil pH
Leaves	30–100:1	3–6 months	3–6 inches	Collection costs only	9	Possible pests, possible weed seed if improperly collected, best if shredded and aged (leaf mold)	
Bark Mulch	100–400:1	1–2 years	3–4 inches		6	Breaks down very slowly, but produces great soil over time, shredding/grinding increases decomposition significantly	Note, overreliance on tree based mulches can alter your soil's bacterial/fungal balance, leading to plant health problems for annuals.
Ramial Chipped Wood	30–100:1	3–6 months	3–6 inches		10	Excellent mulch for buildng soil quickly, breaks down rapidly	
Woods chip, small or fine	300–500:1	8–12 months	3–6 inches	.04–.08	10	Trash and other debris contamination. If using certain types of seeding and other equipment, won't work well with wood chip mulches	Note, for all wood chips, addition of sufficient green matter reduces their durability by one third to one half and will also alter their C/N ratio.
Wood chips, medium	300–500:1	12–18 months	3–6 inches	.04–.08	10		
Wood chips, large	300–500:1	16–24 months	3–6 inches	.04–.08	5	**Use in paths, animal bedding, or in compost, not generally recommended for mulching a growing bed**	
Wood chips/chunks, very large with small diameter branches, etc.	300–500:1	24–36 months	–		2	**Will need rechipped or otherwise processed, not appropriate as a mulch**	

All tree based mulch materials have the danger of containing allopathic chemicals – chemicals that are harmful or that inhibit the germination or growth of other plants

Grass and Plant Based Mulches

		Durability	Thickness to apply		Desirability	Do's and Don'ts
Straw	40-100:1	6-9 months	6-12 inches	.03-.10/square foot	7	Herbicide contamination danger; stays in place better when chopped but reduces durability some, habitat for larger pests species
Hay (note, particular species are more durable and higher in fertility than others, such as alfalfa, while often being lower in weed seed load)	25:1	4-8 months	6-12 inches	.06-.15/square foot	5	Herbicide contamination danger, stays in place better than straw, weed seed risk moderate to very high
Grass clipping	10-25:1	1-2 months	2-4 inches	Collect costs only	4	Herbicide and pesticide contamination, Grass and weed seed contamination, phosphorous overload risk, tends to mat, short duration
Cover Crops, crimped and rolled or flail mowed	Depends on varieties and timing of crop kill	3-6 months	Varies	Depends on seed costs, types used, equipment, and scale of operation	10	Difficult to plant into unless transplanting or using specilized planting equipment, if not mowed, crimped, or rolled properly, plants may bounce back and regrow

Miscellaneous Organic Mulches

		Durability	Thickness to apply		Desirability	Do's and Don'ts
Newspaper	175-200:1	2-4 months	1/2-1 inch	Collect costs only	4	Concern over inks, low durability, messy, best under another mulch and in paths. Closer to plants, apply thinner layer
Cardboard	600:1	3-6 months	1-2 inches	Collect costs only	10	Remove all tape, staples, stick with low ink, best used in paths or under newly established beds with non-root crops
Coffee Grounds	20-25:1	4-8 months	1-2 inches	Collect costs only	5	Limited use for pest deterrence around certain plants/crops, generally not recommended as mulch, excellent addition to compost and vermicompost
Compost	20-30:1	3-6 months	2 inches	Collect costs only	7	May decrease or increase weed issues, care must be taken to maintain nutrient balance in soil

Note, for all mulches, generally the further south you go, the shorter their durability. The further north you go, the longer their durability. Fall cover crops that are mowed or crimped/rolled on top of mulches will hasten their breakdown over Winter.

John's Guide to Using Organic Wood Chip Mulches

What is it?	Age	How do I tell?	How do I use it?
Fresh Wood Chips	Fresh to about 12 weeks old	Wood will retain natural color and smell. May contain fresh green material like leaves, needles, etc. Piles will generate heat and steam from composting action.	Reserve for paths or compost, but best to age before use. If you are trying to suppress weeds in paths, fresh chips allopathic properties MAY help with some weed species
Aged Wood Chips	12 weeks old to about 12 months	Wood chips no longer retain smell or color of original species. Leafy green matter is decomposed. May begin to show signs of mycellium/mold/fungal colonization. Pile no longer produces heat/steam.	Good general mulch for most crops, especially peppers, cabbages, tomatoes, cucumbers, and the like
Rotted wood chips	Over 12 months old	Pile is thoroughly colonized by fungi and molds. Little to no identifiable green material. Wood chip structure is often soft, pliable. Parts of pile resemble soil. Pile is cold.	Especially good as a mulch for root crops, like potatoes, sweet potatoes or for enriching poorer areas of soil around crops like peppers, cucumbers, and the like. Also, good for paths.
Leaf Mold	Best after 6 or so months	To make leaf mold, shred fresh leaves. Shredded leaves can be applied in Fall, or piled to hasten decomposition for use in Spring	Great to mulch overwinter crops with in Fall, such as garlic. Good general purpose mulch in Spring, but will give out by mid to late Summer.
Ramial Chipped Wood	Use as soon as made	Made from branches in leaf less than 2.5 inches in diameter. Needs to be well chipped to break down properly	If well chipped, excellent for almost all crops. Will need replenished if applied in early Spring by mid to late Summer.

Note – With rooted wood chips, I generally follow with an aged wood chip mulch a few weeks later

Man Made Mulches Summary

Type	Benefits	Drawbacks	Cost	Labor
Black Plastic	Warms soil, conserves water, reduces weeding, improves yields for heat loving crops. Also, reduces soil splash (dirt and soil knocked up upon plant leaves and fruits by heavy rains), helping reduce transmission of plant diseases	Soil may stick to plastic, leading to significant soil loss each season without additional labor, creates large amounts of plastic pollution, large amount of labor at front and back end of season to install and remove, requires installation of irrigation. Hard to install without specialized equipment. Some pests thrive underneath it.	Very low	Moderate to high
Geotextiles (Ground cover/landscape fabric)	Similar to black plastic, but far more durable. Also, much easier to install without specialized equipment.	Similar to black plastic. Concern over chemical leaching. May require occasional sanitation because of plant diseases that build up in fabric.	Very low	Moderate
IRT Mulch	Similar to black plastic, but heats soil more quickly by allowing certain light wavelengths to pass through	Not suitable for more southernly climates, as it will create too much heat in the soil unless covered or removed, adding additional labor	Low	Moderate to high
Metal	Most durable of all mulches	Sharp edges, must be weighed down or very dangerous in wind, habitat for both mid line predators and pests.	Low	Low
Tire Crumb Mulch	Available free or cheap	I cannot recommend – numerous studies show immense dangers to tire crumb mulches, including hazardous chemical outgassing and presence of heavy metals that leach into and build up in soil	Low	Moderate
Carpet	Available free and in abundance	I cannot recommend - carpet contains a number of problematic chemicals that leaching into the soil	Free	Low
Stone	Great for certain perennials in permanent beds	If decide to change/remove, massive pain in the butt.	High	Moderate to High

Comparison of Organic, Living, and Landscape Materials

	Organic Mulches	Living mulches/Cover crops	Landscape Fabric/Plasticulture
Timing sensitive	No, can be applied anytime, but most effective before weed emergence and establishment	Timing is critical	Yes, best applied before weed emergence and establishment
For dry areas	More preferable	less preferable	More preferable
For wet areas	Less preferable	more preferable	Less preferable
Attract pollinators and beneficials	No	Yes	No
Cool soil, reducing plant stress	Yes	Yes	Warms soil in spring and fall, may cause
Labor to establish	Moderate	Low	Moderate to high, includes removal
Skill level to use	Low	Moderate	Moderate, requires drip irrigation
Builds soil organic matter	Yes	Yes	No
Helps remove excess moisture from soils	No	Yes	No
Protects ground from compaction from	Yes	Yes	No
Adds nutrients to soil	Yes	Yes	No

Animal Manures

	What is it high in?	What is it low in?	NPK	C/N	What is it good for?	What are the dangers?
Worm Castings	Varies by inputs, generally, excellent for micronutrients as well as macros	Varies by input, but good general fertilizer and soil amendment	See note	20:1	Slow release	When properly made, none
BSF Castings	Varies by inputs	Varies by inputs	5.0-3.0-2.0	20:1	BSF bio-remediate inputs by removing heavy metals (which means if you are using low quality inputs, you shouldn't feed them to your animals!)	When properly made, none
Bat Guano	High in calcium, good for a wide range of minerals		10.0-3.0-1.0	8-15:1	Excellent source of nitrogen, but watch the phosphorous	Generally, none, but you see why getting bats on your property is a good idea if you can collect the manure!
Rabbit	Nitrogen and phosphorous	Depends on feed	(2.5-7)-(1.5-3)-.5	*	Great for corn and other needy crops, cold composts	Generally none
Chicken		*	1.1-6.0 0.5-4.0 0.5-3.0	*	Great for corn and other needy crops	Easy to self-produce
Pig		*		*	Great for corn and other needy crops	Parasites
Horse		*	0.5-2.5 0.3-2.5 0.5-3.0	*		Grass and weed seed, possible herbicide pass through and contamination
Cow		*	0.5-2.0 0.2-0.9 0.5-1.5	*		
Goat		*	?	*		
Lamb		*	1.0-4.0 1.0-2.5 1.0-3.0	*		

* Almost all animal manures carry pathogen risks. So, all must either undergo proper thermophilic composting or proper aging before use. Especially if you are selling produce, these rules are non-negotiable. Animal manure fertilizer values vary substantially in real life, because of time of year, animal diet, and especially, bedding selection. * IF at all possible, it is best to get fertility tests from makers of compost, especially worm, to better estimate what you are receiving nutrient wise. Also, some compost makers, especially worm, can adjust their process to better tailor their final product to your needs.

If animals are fed good quality feed and supplements, especially kelp and similar, their manures will contain a fair amount of trace minerals and nutrients.

Keeping Paths Weed Free

Approach or type	Effectiveness	Other Notes
Keep bare, light cultivation	Moderately effective to effective	Increases labor, exposes bare soil
Newspaper + organic mulch	Moderately effective, depending on types of weeds and grasses present	Somewhat labor intensive to lay lots of newspaper, concern of chemicals in dyes and inks
Cardboard + organic mulch (straw or wood chips)	Very effective, superior weed suppression to newspaper	My preferred path maintenance method, especially when starting new areas. In fall, a cover crop can be sown into the paths
Metal mulch	Very effective, excellent if short on time or materials for options 2 or 3	Watch your toes! Ensure metal is thoroughly secured
Cover crop alone	Effective	While crop is becoming established, care must be taken to not damage the cover crop, timing is crucial
Organic mulch + cover crop	Very effective if established at proper time for most weeds	Timing is crucial as is proper mix selection
Leave in grass	Requires careful management and mowing	Certain species will easily spread back into adjoining beds if they are not under plastic or landscape fabric
Rocks or gravel	Somewhat effective	Not recommended, save for very small spaces with raised, permanent beds. Rock is very hard to remove and sometimes, very hard to weed
Rocks or gravel + steam weeding or boiling water	Effective, steam or water weeding is the most appropriate and effective way to weed such spaces	See above

Fence Line Comparison

Technique	Cost per linear foot	Durability	Effectiveness	Coverage	Labor Cost
Metal Mulch	.50-1.50	10-20 years	95-100%	Covers both sides	Very low
Organic mulch (straw, wood chips, etc.)	.10-.20	6-9 months	60-80%	Need to do each side individually	Moderate
Mechanial Weeding (weed whacker)	$3-5/per hour plus labor costs	7-14 days	95-100%	Need to do each side individually	Moderate to high
Steam or flame	.05 cents	15-45 days	95-100%	Possibly both, but most likely each side individually	Moderate
Horticultural vinegar and salt	.05-.10	30-90 days	70-90%	Possibly both	Moderate to high

Cover Crops

	Deep Roots, good natural tillage	Early Spring	Summer	Early to mid-fall	Great animal forage	Frost/winter kill	Weed Suppression (fast growth, dense cover)	Pollinator attractor
Grains and pseudo-grains								
Buckwheat		x	x	x	x	x	x	x
Rye Grass		x	x	x			x	
Oat				x	x		x	
Legumes and other nitrogen fixers								
Clover		x	x	x	x		x	x
Cowpea		x	x		x	x	x	
Avirsaki (Forage pea)		x	x		x	x	x	x
Alfalfa	x		x	x	x		x	x
Vetch		x	x	x			x	
Other								
Daikon	x	x	x	x	x	x		
Turnip	x	x	x	x				

Crop by Crop Weed Control

Crop	Suggested	Also effective	Watch out for
Asparagus	Organic mulch	Cover crops or living mulches coupled with organic mulches work well between beds	If bed area is overly wet, mulch can led to rot/disease issues with plants. After harvest, mulching plants with a very rich compost (such as one that contains chicken manure) can help "burn" out weeds while providing fertilizer for next season's harvest.
Basil	Occultation or solarization followed by transplanting and light organic mulch. Careful with tight spacing because of disease issues.	Geotextile or black plastic mulch, can also do cultivation.	As a warm season plant, basil benefits from any technique that helps bring up soils temps early season
Perennial herbs (Sage, Oregano, thyme)	Living and/or organic mulches. These are especially good to do in large pots/earth boxes so you can move indoors or to sheltered locations for season extension or year round growing	Cultivation between plants	Perennials benefit from wood chip based mulches, as it helps create soil conditions more suited to their needs
Cilantro	Occultation followed by direct seeding or transplants, once plants are established organic mulch	Geotextile	Germinates poorly at cooler soil temperatures, so occultation increases germination rates. Cilantro tends to "bolt," so keeping soil temperatures cool through organic mulches or living mulches and planting bolt resistant varieties in warmer locations helps extend harvest
Other annual herbs (dill, parsley)	When direct seeding, first occultation or solarization, then seed, and once plants are established, light organic mulch, especially rotted shredded straw or leaf mold	Cultivation between rows, geotextile or black plastic	
Beans, bush	Tight planting pattern, excellent to plant along the outside edges of potato and other crop beds. Will grow through light mulch easily and tolerate moderately heavy mulch once established.	Cultivation between rows	
Beans, pole	Organic mulch and/or living mulch understory. Tight planting also helps.	Cultivation between rows	
Beets	Occultation followed by direct seeding or transplants, once plants established organic mulch	Cultivation between rows or geotextile	Beets are sometimes hard to get to germinate. Transplanting allows a significant headstart on weeds especially when soil temps are cooler. Like carrots, can use occultation tarp to help improve germination.
Brocolli, cabbage, cauliflower, kale and similar	Organic mulch, especially shredded straw or wood chips, works very good post occultation. Tight patterns also work very well to reduce weed pressure. Solarizing pre–fall planting works excellently as well.	Geotextile or plastic mulch	Floating row cover is often used to control cabbage worm for this family of crops, so make sure that your weed and pest control approach "fit" together. Also note, it is very easy to forgot to check for weeds once the rowcover is in place!
Carrots and parsnips	Occultation followed by light cultivation or flaming to create stale or false seed bed. Intercropping to take up space until carrots or parsnips are established	For fall planting, solarization	Sometimes hard to germinate – using an occultation tarp late winter/early spring to warm soil and leaving on seeded beds until carrots emerge can improve rates subtantially.
Chard and other greens	Geotextile or shredded straw, RCW, or fine, well rotted wood chip mulch. Dense seeding is very important (3 rows per foot!)	Occultation followed by light cultivation or flaming to create stale of false seed bed. Dense planting is very important (3 rows per foot).	
Corn	Mulch, especially well rotted chicken litter sawdust/wood chip mulch or similar		
Cucumbers	Organic or living mulch understory (clovers and similar plants that are under 12 inches in height)	Geotextile or plastic mulch	Some pests like to live in the mulch, especially geotextile and plastic, but also in organic as well. Pests in geo or plastic mulch can be hard to manage.

Crop	Recommendation	Alternative	Notes
Fennel	Organic mulch, especially once plants are established. Stale seed bed to plant into, cultivation until plants are ready for mulch.	Geotextile or plastic mulch	
Garlic	Organic mulch, especially leaf mold or shredded leaves or well rotted wood chips	Cultivation between rows	Since garlic gets planted in the fall, we solarize garlic beds late summer for fall planting and immediately mulch. The beds are easy to manage until after the following early summer's garlic harvest.
Lettuce	Occultation followed by light cultivation or flaming to create stale or false seed bed then followed by a fine organic mulch (shredded straw or leaves, or rotted, small size wood chips) once plants are established (either by seed or transplant). Tight planting pattern helps immensely with weed suppression.	Geotextile or plastic mulch	Geotextile preferred over plastic mulch, as you can reuse it for many years. Note that certain diseases can build up in the fabric, so occasionally sanitation may be required.
Melons	Organic or living mulch, especially post occultation or solarization	Geotextile	
Onions	Occultation followed by light cultivation or flaming to create stale or false seed bed then followed by organic mulch	Geotextile or plastic mulch	Geotextile preferred over plastic mulch, as you can reuse it for many years and it does very well with onions
Peas	Occultation followed by tight planting and light organic mulch of straw or rotted wood chips	Geotextile or plastic mulch	
Peppers	Occultation or solarization followed by organic and/or living mulch.	Geotextile or plastic mulch	Because peppers are a heat loving plant, in cooler climates many growers prefer geotextile or black plastic to extend the season and increase yields.
Potatoes	Organic mulch, especially wood chips	Cultivation in between rows	In field trials, straw tends to produce more pest damage than wood chip mulches. If the straw is well shredded and rotted, the damage and difference between the two mulches is greatly reduced.
Raddish	Good to intercrop with other crops, such as lettuce, carrot, fennel, and more		
Raspberry and Blackberry	Rotted wood chip mulch, especially paired with a living understory of clover or similar plants	None	These plants natural habitat is forest edge land, aka, a land covered in natural, wood based organic mulches and some low growing, spreading plants.
Spinach	Organic mulches, generally on the finer side (shredded straw, small wood chips or RCW) especially once plants are established (3-4 weeks after direct seeding, 7-14 days after transplanting)	Cultivation in between rows, geotextile or black plastic	Spinach prefers cooler temperatures, so organic and living mulches coupled with planting to create shade as season goes on can extend your window of harvest
Strawberries	Shredded straw or well rotted wood chip mulch	Geotextile or plastic mulch	
Summer Squash	Organic mulch, especially wood chips, especially post occultation or solarization	Geotextile or plastic mulch	Some pests like to live in the mulch, especially geotextile and plastic. Pests can be excluded using floating row cover until the flowering stage, then various controls will be needed once plants are uncovered.
Sweet potatoes	Organic mulch, especially wood chips, especially post occultation or solarization to help warm the soil. Sweet potatoes prefer warm soil temperatures, so anything that helps warm the soil earlier may let you plant sooner.	IRE plastic in northing climates, plastic mulch in still semi-cool mid latitude locations	Raised mounds work best, both to increase yields and reduce pest pressure, especially from ground dwelling rodents. Mulches increase yields, but if rodent pressure is an issue, can exacerbate the problem without proper management.
Tomatoes, including cherry and grape	Organic mulch and/or living mulch, especially post occultation or solarization to warm soil before transplanting.	Geotextile or plastic mulch	It is very important to not allow bare soil beneath tomatoes, as it can quickly spread disease
Winter squash (including pumpkins)	Organic or living mulch, especially post occultation or solarization	Geotextile or plastic mulch	Similar to summer squash, mulch can exacerbate pest issues, and geotextile or plastic mulch can make some pests hard to control.

John's Quick Guide to Common Compostables and Garden Inputs

	What is it high in?	What is it low in?	NPK	C/N	What is it good for?	What are the dangers?
Cardboard	Carbon.	Everything else	0-0-0	600:1	Under mulch, in compost (both regular and worm)	Generally, none. Stay with low to no ink. Remove all tape and staples.
Coffee Grounds	Carbon, phosphorus, potassium, magnesium and copper	Calcium, zinc, manganese and iron	(.3-2)-(3 -2.0)-(.5-.7)	20-25:1	As a thin mulch to deter slugs and other garden pests, best in compost (both regular and worm)	Generally, none. Best married to a calcium rich input in compost (lime, oyster shell, eggshells, etc.)
COIR	Carbon, iron, boron copper, zinc, manganese		.5-1-1.8	80-120:1	Use in compost, especially worm, plant starts, as soil amendment	Make sure reputable brand, must be desalinated
Pitch Produce	Depends on quality and type.	Depends on quality and type.	Varies, especially seasonally	10-20:1	Animal feed, additive to compost	Agricultural chemical residues, plant pathogens and diseases
Leaves	Carbon	Everything	1.0-(.2 to .4) -(.2-.4)	30-80:1	Compost (both regular and worm), mulch, some species are low in calcium, so to hasten breakdown add some source	Allopathic species, possible pests
Peatmoss	Carbon	Everything	.5-0-0	50-60:1	Good for lowering soil pH and adding organic matter	Generally, none
Straw	Carbon, Potassium	Everything else	.5-.2-(.6-2)	40-100:1	Animal bedding, mulch	Herbicide and pesticide contamination, Grass and weed seed contamination
Grass Clippings	Phosphorous, nitrogen	Varies depending on soil and species	4-.5-2	15-25:1	Personally, I dislike grass clippings. I prefer to let animals do my mowing!	Herbicide and pesticide contamination, Grass and weed seed contamination, phosphorous overload danger
Comfrey	Generally, moderate to high in many things	Varies depending on soil and species, but scavenges even in poor soils	(3-4) - (1) - (5-8)		Note the very high potassium!	Generally none.
Cover Crops, Legume	Carbon and Nitrogen	Cycles what is present in soil	(2-5) - 0 - 0		Vital in organic systems to raise N without adding PK	Takes practice to do well.
Eggshells	Calcium Magnesium	Everything else	1.2 0.4 0.3		Good addition to compost, especially vermicompost	Pathogen risk
Mushroom Compost	Carbon, calcium, magnesium, iron	Varies	(1.42 – 2.05)-(0.45 – 0.69) –(1.93 – 2.58)	20:1	Good soil amendment	Generally none.
Wood Ash	Carbon, Phosphorous, Potassium	Varies, mostly low to very low	0.0-1-3	25:1	Some pests (like slugs and snails) dislike wood ashes. Similar to coffee grounds, can be used to discourage	Generally none if you are burning only wood. Wood ash + pee makes an excellent fertilizer!

Weed Control Cost Comparison

	Durability	Depth to apply	Cost per square foot	Cost per square foot per year	Notes
Occultation	3–5 years	N/A	Silage Tarp – .06–.08	.02–.03	Proper ground prep and storage will extend life of plastic, but as soon as it shows signs of becoming brittle, dispose of it immediately
Solarization	2–3 years	N/A	6 mil – 0.15–0.20	.05–.07	Same as above
Forced Germination					
Ramial Chipped Wood	3–6 months	3–6 inches	Most likely will need to make yourself		Generally, hard to find and source
Woods chip, small or fine	8–12 months	3–6 inches	.04–.08	.04–.08	For wood chips, I am estimating a price of $5.00–$10 per cubic yard, which covers approximately 80 square feet at 4 inches deep
Wood chips, medium	12–18 months	3–6 inches	.04–.08	.02–.06	
Wood chips, large	16–24 months	3–6 inches	.04–.08	.02–.04	

For solarization and occultation, above cost estimates do not include shipping costs!

Solarization Guide

	Solarization will take more time if...	Solarization will take less time if...
Slope	North and west	South and east
Shade	More	Less
Season	Spring and Fall, almost impossible before and after equinoxes	Summer, especially 30 days before and after Solstice
Sunlight	Intermittent (partly or mostly cloudy)	Partly or mostly sunny
Soil Moisture	Water logged or overly dry	Moist/damp
Location	Farther north	Farther south
Soil type	Clay	Sand, loam
Size of area	Smaller the area/tarp	Larger the area/tarp

Simple Steps to Solarize

If necessary mow area thoroughly

Clear of any debris that can damage tarp

Ensure proper moisture, water if necessary

Apply tarp

Check temps

Remove when ready

Simple Steps to Occultate

If necessary mow area thoroughly

Clear of any debris that can damage tarp

Ensure proper moisture, water if necessary

Apply tarp

Check temps

Remove when ready

Solarization compared to Occultation

	Solarization	Occultation
Reduces weeds	Yes, excellent	Yes, excellent
Reduces weed seed bank beyond mere germination	Yes, excellent	Possibly
Reduces pests	Yes, excellent to moderate	Possibly, little to moderate impact
Reduces pathogens	Yes, moderate to excellent	No
Time frame	As little as 7-14 days	Minimum six weeks
No till cover crop compatible	Yes, excellent	Yes, excellent
Impact on soil biology	Generally, slightly positive to slightly negative net impact	Unknown
Best time?	Around summer solstice, but depends on location	Any time during the growing season, as well as over the winter in some locations
Other notes	Larger areas are more effective than smaller areas and beds	Little to no loss of effectiveness on small plot or even single bed sizes

When compostable materials are added to the soil before solarization, the process is called biosolarization.

This increases the effectiveness of solarization, while also mitigating any possible negative soil biology impacts and improving soil biology substantially post-solarization.

Tree Species Guide

Aromatics   Cedar, Pine, Eucalyptus, and any woods with strong smells or which essential oils, cleaners, or similar things are derived from

Allopathics   Walnut (Juglandaceae/juglans) Family – walnut, pecan, hickory

Maple (mild) and pine

While the above are the most common, some other trees and shrubs are mildly allopathic, but usually do not pose a threat to garden plants

Animal Danger   red maple, oak leaves, box elder, leaves chokecherry and black walnut, cedar and pine

Durability

	Longer	Shorter
Species	Locust, cypress, redwood, red cedar, Osage orange, oak	Poplar, maple,
Size of chip	Larger, coarser	Smaller, finer
Time of year	Late Fall, Winter, early Spring	Summer, early Fall
Part of tree	Trunk, heartwood	Branches
Amount of Green Matter	Less	More

Dealing with aromatic and allopathic compounds in tree based mulches

Three to six months of proper aging or composting will remove aromatic and allopathic compounds. This does not apply in hugelkulture systems or to full sized, unchipped branches and other materials. The smaller/finer the chipping of materials and the greater the amount of green material, the faster aromatic and allopathic compounds will break down.

About the Author

John Moody is the founder of Whole Life Services and Whole Life Buying Club, author of *The Elderberry Book* and *The Frugal Homesteader Handbook*. He and his family have been involved with farming, food, health, and homesteading for over a decade. John is a well-known speaker at numerous conferences and events around the country, such as the Mother Earth News Fairs. He, Jessica, and their five rambunctious kids try to keep the farm and homestead together until the cows come home on 35 acres in Kentucky.

CPSIA information can be obtained
at www.ICGtesting.com
Printed in the USA
LVHW092233300919
632709LV00010B/986/P